Day X

The world situation in the light of the
Second Coming of Christ

by Kurt Koch, Th.D.

KREGEL PUBLICATIONS
Grand Rapids, Michigan 49501

All Rights Reserved. Translated from the German and published by Evangelizations Publishers, West Germany, 1967. Published in the United States of America by Kregel Publications, a division of Kregel, Inc., P.O. Box 2607, Grand Rapids, Michigan 49501

Library of Congress Catalog Card No. 70-160688

ISBN 0-8254-3005-4

Printed in the United States of America

CONTENTS

Christus ante portas	5
Time is Short	7
A. Characteristic Signs of the Present Age	9
I. The Dethronement of the White Man	12
1. The End of Colonialism	12
2. The Decreasing Impulse of Missionary Work	14
3. Racial Hatred	17
II. The Advance of the Coloured Peoples	21
1. Ascendancy in the Birth Rate	21
2. Ascendancy in Missionary Advance	24
3. The Flood of Occultism	26
III. Dangers of the World	29
1. Political Encirclement	30
2. The Hunger Catastrophe of the Last Days	34
3. Radioactivity and the Fear of the Atom	38
4. The Breakdown of Mental Health in the White Race	41
5. Natural Disasters	43
IV. The Breaking Down of Standards	45
1. The Break-up of Family Life	46
2. The Wave of Sex	48
3. The Wave of Addiction	50
4. The Breakthrough of Lawlessness	53
5. Indifference to Justice	54
6. The Abandoning of Biblical Standards and Church Ordinances	57
V. The Growing Standardization of Thought and Behaviour	60
1. The Bombardment of the Unconscious by Mass Media	60
2. Standardization in Politics	64
3. The Idea of Religious Unity	68
VI. The Growing Radicalism of Intellectual Movements	73
1. Humanism	74
2. Neo-Rationalist Theology	76
3. The New "Art"	85
VII. Israel	93

B. Drawing Conclusions ... 101
    I. A warning against hasty conclusions ... 102
    II. The general mobilization of the enemy ... 104
    III. How does the world react to eschatological events? ... 107
    IV. How will Christ's Church survive the turmoil of the Last Days? ... 113
    V. The final victory is the Lord's ... 119
    VI. Who will take part? ... 124

*God has fixed **a day**
on which he will judge the world.*
Acts 17, 31

*The **day of the Lord**
will come like
a thief in the night.*
1 Thessalonians 5, 2

*The **day** is at hand.*
Romans 13, 12

Christus ante portas

It was during the time of Daniel that Belshazzar prepared his great feast. All the presidents of the provinces of Babylon and the satraps and governors were invited.

The feast was to be a demonstration of his power. But he also considered himself to be the religious head of the nation. He had therefore called for the vessels of silver and gold which had been taken from the temple in Jerusalem to be brought. "The God of Israel can do nothing to prevent my wives and concubines from drinking from these vessels," he boasted.

But this desecration was not enough. The ancient text goes on to say, "They drank wine and praised the gods of gold and silver, bronze, iron, wood and stone". This was open defiance and a direct challenge to the unseen world.

The challenge was accepted. The fingers of a man's hand wrote upon the wall. Daniel was brought before the king. His interpretation spoke of judgement.

Even while the feast had been in process the nation's dread enemy, the Medes and Persians, had been advancing towards the city of Babylon.

In the palace the unsuspecting people continued their feasting until they were suddenly startled by the cry, "The Medes and Persians are at the gates!" That very night Belshazzar the king was slain . . .

Two hundred years later we find Rome ruling the Mediterranean area with a rod of iron. As Hannibal grew up in Carthage he absorbed the hatred around him against Rome. "Will my time come?" he asked himself. It came. In 218 B. C. he began his famous trek across the Alps. His fame spread as victory followed victory. In 211 B. C. he reached Rome. "Hannibal ante portas — Hannibal is at the gates", was the cry of the dismayed inhabitants. Their false sense of security had been suddenly shattered.

We are again living in such a time. The only difference is that we are entering the last stages of the world's history.

In 1969 I was speaking at a meeting in New York. A friend there told me of the action the police had taken against a Protestant church in the neighbourhood. During a certain carnival or festival, there had been an exhibition of pornographic pictures in the church hall. The police had gone there and had forbidden them to continue the exhibition. Churches going the way of Sodom and Gomorrah! Where will enormities like this end? The judge is standing at the doors!

In May of the same year I received an invitation to speak at a German youth group. There was a red flag flying over the building. A picture of Lenin together with various communist slogans decorated the walls of the room. A young girl who was studying theology led the discussion. She had just taken her final examinations. Quite suddenly she called out, "Jesus was a homosexual!" I sprang up. "That's blasphemy," I cried. "I can't stay here any longer." I left the room at once. A young man called out after me, "And Mary was a prostitute as well!" — the end of theology! The despised one, the one they pronounced dead, the unseen one, the coming one is standing at the doors!

It is towards him that this book points.

Time is Short

In the autumn of 1966 the World Congress on Evangelism met in Berlin. Altogether almost 2,000 people took part — delegates, representatives of the press, and committee members — from over a hundred countries. Unanimously chosen as honorary chairman was Dr. Billy Graham. The nine-day conference ended on November 4th, about the time of Dr. Graham's 48th birthday.

In his final address he said, "Humanly speaking my strength will be sufficient for about 10 more years of evangelistic work. When we consider the world situation, it is also possible that the doors for evangelism will only be open for ten years more. In the next ten years decisive events will probably take place, such as Christianity has never encountered in all her history."

Then Billy Graham told of an audience with the former Federal Chancellor of West Germany, Dr. Adenauer. "After greeting me," he said, "this great German spontaneously asked me, 'Dr. Graham, do you believe in the resurrection of the dead?' 'Of course I do.' 'So do I,' replied the experienced politician, 'otherwise I should despair. World history is taking a terrible course.'"

This short conversation between the great politician, who has since died, and Billy Graham, is symptomatic. It throws a significant light on the times we live in. The evangelists gathered in the Congress Hall listened with rapt attention and inward assent to what Billy Graham had to say.

This was also noticeable in the closing prayer meeting. Never in my life have I experienced such a time of prayer. In this Congress Hall, normally given over to every kind of spirit and to worldly meetings of all sorts, there were now 1,200 men on their knees at prayer. The Spirit of God brooded over this meeting. There was no noise, no disturbance in the form of undisciplined interjections and emotional excitement. Rather it was the "still, small voice" as of old on Mount Horeb (1 Kings 19:12b). As we arose from our knees, we all knew it was the Lord who had met with us. Many men — I among them — wiped tears from their eyes.

Time is short — with this thought Billy Graham began his final address. Time is hurrying to its close — that is also my theme in this book. Somewhere in the world — I do not recall the name of the place — I found a stone table on which were engraved the words "It's later than you think". The day is at hand.

A. Characteristic Signs of the Present Age

To introduce this subject I will recount an experience I had a few years ago. I was visiting a number of mission fields at the time, among others that of the Swiss Indian Mission in Peru. Mr. Hauser, one of the missionaries, joined me for a trip from the mission base near Pucallpa to one of the outstations. On the way we passed through part of the Amazon jungle. Suddenly he stopped, and pointed to a massive tree. There, on the branches of this jungle giant, were 20 or 30 vultures sitting in a row like pearls on a string.

"Do you know what that means?" asked my companion. "Not hard to guess," I replied. In prophesying His return, Jesus said, "Wherever the body is, there the vultures will be gathered together" (Matt. 24:28). So it was here. As we went on our way, we saw the carcass of an animal lying near the tree.

This example illustrates a fact of very great importance. This is that definite, observable happenings enable us to draw conclusions about hidden realities and background events. This means that the things in the foreground, which we are able to take in, are symptoms and indications of something else. Such a relation between the seen and the unseen is found not only in nature, but also in the spiritual realm.

In this book we shall be taking the symptoms to be seen in our present time, and from them drawing conclusions about the unseen aspects of this age. In doing this we shall be attempting to discover the true nature of the present world situation. The object of this undertaking is to reveal the basic pattern of current events. We are not trying to make a superficial and onesided assessment, or to paint everything in black and white. Nor do we want a view of current events conditioned by our momentary viewpoint. We will gladly leave it to psychologists, philosophers and journalists to make a secular analysis of our age. These observers of world events sometimes have a remarkable ability for hitting nails on the head. Yet their analyses do not go beyond a certain limit. This means that they have a grave and fundamental deficiency. They have no other points of reference than those dictated by human reason. Without the illumination of the Holy Spirit, and without the biblical gift of knowledge and the discernment of spirits, every assessment of our times must be inaccurate and distorted. In 1 Corinthians 2:14 the apostle Paul makes it unmistakably clear where the limit lies: the unspiritual man does not receive what comes from the Spirit of God.

In order to recognise the nature of the times we live in, it is an absolute necessity at the outset to know the Scriptures — and that without the destructive influence of biblical criticism. To see through the surface events of our day to the sinister developments behind the scenes, one must first have been broken in spirit, touched by the hand of God. Otherwise one can go no further than making a purely outward assessment. The Holy Spirit alone leads into all truth, not the sharpened intellect of an unconverted analyst and philosopher.

In the chapters which follow an attempt will be made to discover, without extravagant speculation,

Signs of the Present Age

the character of our day and age. The Holy Scriptures with their prophecies are our authoritative guide, even though we may not mention them specifically at every point. Where the Bible is not acknowledged as the absolute authority in matters of faith, hopeless mistakes will be made in the interpretation of the present time. Only Scripture tells us clearly how to proceed.

Two important instructions of this sort are, for instance, given us by Jesus Himself. In Matthew 16:3 He reproached the Pharisees, "You know how to interpret the appearance of the sky, but you cannot interpret the signs of the times." And in Matthew 24:36 the Lord said to His disciples, "But of that day and hour no one knows, not even the angels of heaven, but the Father only."

These two verses mark the limits for our expectation of the return of Christ.

On the one hand, to try and calculate the day and hour of the last things is to fall into extravagant speculation.

He who on the other hand ignores the signs of the times, and cannot interpret them, belongs to those who sleep and are blind.

In this book care will be taken to avoid both dangers. We shall make no calculations. Even what we quoted from Billy Graham has for us no numerical significance. But the hour urgently demands that we recognise the signs of the present time.

The material we shall be considering has not been collected out of missionary literature, but direct from the mission fields. The impressions recorded here were formed in visiting over 400 mission stations in about 90 countries. The first dominant symptom of our time is:

I. THE DETHRONEMENT OF THE WHITE MAN

The world of nations has become a seething cauldron. In South Vietnam rebels are constantly pinning notices to the walls of houses, demanding "Yankee go home". In Hong Kong, Red Chinese agents are stirring up the masses to break off every contact with the Western world, and especially with England. Here it is "Tommy go home". Not only is the British Empire coming to an end, but it seems that the days of the Commonwealth are numbered. France has suffered the same fate in Algeria and Indo-China. This unrest all over the world has only one purpose: to destroy the white man's influence. Let us outline three symptoms which mark this development.

1. *The End of Colonialism*

The work of centuries of white colonialism is coming to an end. The white man has educated the underdeveloped peoples. They have learnt much from his discoveries, his science and technology, and also from his culture. Now they have come of age and demand their independence.

The pupils are growing stronger than their teacher. The white man is losing ground and being put in his place. In some places this has resulted in rough treatment and hasty decisions.

When I was travelling through Africa I heard of a power station, which had been built by white people and was manned by white engineers. In keeping with the motto of "Africa for the Africans", the European engineers were sent home. One day

Dethronement of the White Man

a repair became necessary. The Africans could not repair the fault. The power station came to a standstill, and the electricity supply for the whole district ceased. The result was that they had to send a telegram to the old engineers, asking them to return.

In Central Africa I heard of a similar incident. The white doctors of a hospital were sent home. The Africans who had up to now worked there as assistants, and whose capabilities extended at the most to the application of bandages and massage, thought their chance had come. When the white men had gone, they proudly called themselves "Doctor". When the first patient with appendicitis came, there was a catastrophe. The so-called "doctors" were of course incapable of carrying out an appendix operation. In relating this story, I do not mean to say that there are no trained and gifted African doctors. There are in fact some who are extremely good at their job.

Even if the coloured peoples often go down blind alleys through over-hasty expulsion of the white man, one can nonetheless see how sick they are of white dominance. They want to shake off this tutelage. Sometimes the white man is only reaping what he has sown. Certainly the coloured peoples have gained much from him. But unfortunately they have also often been exploited. On my travels I heard of some shocking examples of the covetousness and avarice of white businessmen.

Fortunately there are some examples which strike a happier note. In Central Australia great deposits of gold and copper were discovered. Rich fields of precious stones were found as well. To protect the native population from white exploiters with a lust for gold and precious stones, the Australian government has declared these areas reserves for the aboriginal tribes. No white man may enter these restricted areas without government permission. This guarantees for the native tribes the use of their own land's natural treasures. A wise measure of the Australian government!

But now we must ask ourselves a question. What is the significance in world history of this progressive dethronement of the white man, this end of colonialism? To put it more accurately: are we to regard it as an indication of something happening behind the scenes?

Does this development mean nothing more than that the culture and dominance of the white man has reached its zenith, and is now on the decline? There are ethnologists who think so. Or has God put an end to the dominance of the white races, because their sins cry out to heaven? This should earnestly be considered.

At all events, behind this process of decline we can see another development:

Symptom 1   The white races have for 1900 years been the predominant representatives of Christianity. The dethronement of the white man has as its ultimate objective the dethronement also of Christianity. And God allows it.

2. The Decreasing Impulse of Missionary Work

The decline of the white man's power has also struck a blow at Christian missions. The coloured peoples say, "Christianity is the white man's religion! Away with this faith! We have our own

Dethronement of the White Man

religions." Sometimes I heard it expressed in still stronger terms, "What sort of missionaries are they? They give their sanction to the atrocities of the conquerors and exploiters. Are we to accept the white man's God, who allowed them to take away our land and its treasures? What sort of a God is he, if his worshippers treated us like slaves?" It cuts no ice with the coloured people to point out that the missionaries did not approve of the evil deeds of the conquerors.

Christian missionary work is marked today by a shrinking process which has already begun. Great areas which were once covered by the ministry of missions are being lost and coming under other influences. The tendency may be observed by looking at many minor developments. Here are a few examples.

In South Africa a Lutheran church has ceased to exist. The building is now a department store. As a sad memorial of the past, the bell still hangs in the steeple. On another mission field the same thing happened. The congregation dispersed; the church was sold. A great many examples of this sort of thing can be found. Twice I stood before buildings which had been formerly used for gospel meetings. Now they serve other purposes. And this was in a former revival area! Some churches have actually become the tombstones of one-time congregations, although they may be kept in repair at great cost. If the stones of these walls could cry, they would pour out their lament, "Here we once heard the hymns of praise and the prayers of the saints; now there is the peace of a graveyard."

If it be thought that these examples prove little, there is at least food for thought in the ones that follow. They are all developments of the recent past or of the present time.

Red China has sent all missionaries home. A people of 700 million has no permitted Christian church and no regular Christian services. Or we could think of what has happened in the Congo. How many Belgian and American missionaries gave their lives for Jesus Christ there! And who has not heard of the many difficulties in lands of Moslem domination, where work is made well-nigh impossible for Christian missionaries?

The most terrible example of all is the events in the Sudan. The government is in the hands of the Arab ruling class. In the South there are negro villages with a definitely Christian population. These industrious negroes with their upright carriage are a thorn in the flesh for the Arab Moslems. In the spring of 1967 a campaign of annihilation aimed at these people was begun. Their huts, their possessions and their fields are being confiscated. They are being hunted down, set upon, killed — and none of the world powers raises a finger to help these harrassed people. Anyone who is a Christian is without honour, rights or protection in the Sudan.

I had a very slight taste of this myself. When I entered Khartoum I filled in a questionnaire. Shortly afterwards I was arrested. In my bewilderment I asked why. "Pastors, missionaries and Israelis are not wanted here," I was told. I was not even kept long enough to have one meal of bread and water before being loaded on to the next plane and sent packing.

On the basis of Scripture we ask: is not the restriction of missions related to some deeper, underground process? We reply:

Dethronement of the White Man

Symptom 2   There will be a reduction in the sphere of activity for Christian missions. There are movements, systems, nations, and even supernatural powers, for whom Christianity is an offence.

3. Racial Hatred

For several decades the white race has been surrounded by a sea of hostility. For all their differences non-whites are united in one resolve: that if necessary they will stand together against the white man. This racial hatred is so deep-rooted that even a military alliance cannot remove it. An example of this was the murdering of the German missionaries in Manus (South Seas). When the Japanese landed on this island during the 2nd World War and imprisoned the missionaries, the latter protested, "But we are Germans. You are our allies." "First and foremost," replied the Japanese, "you are white men." And in spite of the alliance, the missionaries lost their lives.

Racial hatred is bearing some very poisonous fruit at the present time. In the southern states of the U.S.A. about 10 % of the total population is negro. Their vitality, however, makes up for their lack of numbers. They call themselves the "black power", and demand "black jurisdiction" and "black law". They demand their share of official positions. Certainly the conflict is also concerned with the due rights of the coloured people. But is not the atmosphere to a great extent poisoned by racial hatred?

In South Africa things are still worse. The white government of South Africa certainly goes to great pains to put an end to the continuous racial struggle. But they have not yet succeeded, for the laws, and not least the guilt of the white man, stand in the way of every effort. One or two examples will make it plain how tense the situation is.

A white woman missionary had trouble with her car near a "location" (i.e. dwelling-area of the Bantus). Not far away lived a Christian negro family. The missionary was, however, not allowed by the law of the land to accept the hospitality of these negro Christians. She therefore had to spend the night in the car. If she had stayed just one day in the black family's hut, she would have been expelled from the country.

A white man had an accident in his car. He was badly injured. A negro doctor happened to be driving along the same road. He explained that he was a doctor, showed his doctor's certificate, and offered to help. The white people standing around prevented him from doing so. It is beneath the dignity of a white man to receive treatment from a negro doctor. The man bled to death. They would rather let a man die than accept the help of a negro doctor.

Where is this racial arrogance leading to? One day the whites will have to face a bitter day of reckoning. Their pride threatens to lead to a volcanic outbreak of hatred. The black people have been held under, and their natural self-respect has been wounded. Will they not wreak a terrible vengeance? Will not thousands of white people then lose their lives?

The feeling among the coloured peoples is given expression by the Chinese President Chou En-lai. "The white race," he has said, "constitutes about one-tenth of the world's population. Let us com-

Dethronement of the White Man

pletely annihilate the white man, then we shall be free of him once and for all!" Everyone familiar with Red China realises that the Chinese will try to implement this proposal as soon as they have power enough to do so.

There are leading men who think that the last war this earth sees will be a racial war — coloured against white.

In this connection we may point to one very interesting political development of the last few years. Red China is becoming the natural enemy of Soviet Russia. There are three reasons for this.

First of all there is the matter of population. China is overflowing with people. The area of Siberia on the other side of the border is, on the other hand, thinly populated. It would be the most natural and advantageous direction for Red China to move in. Russia is aware of this. That is why she is trying to secure the Chinese border area by the construction of factories and villages along it. Even the Germans left stranded on the Volga in the 2nd World War were moved into Mongolia.

The second reason for the worsening of relations is the slight difference between white skin and yellow. The Chinese make no bones about it: they say, "The Russians too are whites. Therefore we want nothing to do with them, even if they were once our political comrades, or our military allies in Korea, Indo-China and Vietnam."

The third reason is also a racial one. The Asiatic is more radical and determined when it comes to politics. The Chinese accuse the Russian communists of pandering to the West, and say that they are ready to compromise for the sake of gain.

From my own observation of this development,

I have already for three years been of the opinion that Russia will one day be forced to unite with the West in order to avoid being overrun by the East. It was a confirmation of my opinion to read, as I was writing this chapter, the following headlines in bold type in two newspapers, "Peking reckons with an American-Soviet attack." This change in the structure of the world political situation is so significant that I will quote the relevant section from the front page of the "Stuttgarter Zeitung" of Monday, 12th December, 1966,

> "The Chinese Foreign Minister Chen Yi has expressed bluntly in an interview published by the 'Journal do Brasil' his expectation that the Soviet Union and the United States will one day make a united military attack upon China from the north and south. Moscow policies, he said, were directed towards co-operation with Washington; and China was sure that this aim would find practical expression before very long."

This quotation must not be misunderstood. The point in question is not whether this forecast will be fulfilled or not, but simply the fact that some people are speaking of the possibility of an alliance between the U.S.A. and Russia. In view of the growing intensity of racial hatred, such an alliance is well within the bounds of possibility.

From the biblical point of view, these political and racial confrontations are only covers for a deeper conflict. People whose eyes have been opened for the events of the last days know that the final conflict will not be a racial one. Behind the struggle between the races is the Enemy of God; and this dangerous puller of the wires has far more important designs than to stir up the flame of mere racial prejudice.

Symptom 3 The racial problem is only a camouflage. The Arch-enemy of God is not interested in white, yellow, red, brown and black pigmentations of the skin, but in the Church of Christ, which is to be found predominantly among the white peoples. The prince of darkness wants to isolate and to destroy the Church of the returning Lord.

II. THE ADVANCE OF THE COLOURED PEOPLES

Corresponding to the retreat of the white man, there has been an advance among the coloured peoples. They have extended their territory and gained ground. Red China has, for instance, a secret aim of pushing the Russians back to the Urals. The black people of Africa say openly the white population of South Africa should go back to the countries of their origin — England, Germany, Holland, Scandinavia and France. The Arabs talk of exterminating the Israelis. This planned and painstaking repression of the white man can be illustrated in three ways.

1. *Ascendancy in the Birth Rate*

Population expansion is becoming more and more population explosion, the experts tell us. To put it in plain and simple language, the rapid growth of the human race is leading to overpopulation of the earth. We shall be raising this problem again when the question of feeding the world is discussed; here only one aspect of it will be considered.

During the World Congress on Evangelism in Berlin, a large clock was displayed with a map of the world. Every second a child's head lit up on the huge dial of the clock. This was to signify that once a second a human being is born. By the end of the nine-day congress, the human race had over a million new members.

For the Christian, however, the problem is on a different level. We can consider it first from the denominational point of view. In the U.S.A., for instance, Protestants have an average of two children per family, while the Roman Catholics have four. This means that in fifty years' time the United States will probably have become a predominantly Roman Catholic country.

But much more important than the question of denomination is the question of race; and this includes the problem of other religions.

What of the coloured peoples?

There are some tribes which have few children. The Aborigines in Australia have on the average only two. Their very good health, however, ensures that the tribe continues to exist.

The Fiji islanders have an average of three children per family. Here too the numbers are sufficient to keep the tribe alive.

When we turn to those peoples which make up the greater part of mankind, the picture is entirely different. Today half the population of the world consists of the Indians and the Chinese. Chinese people are to be found not only in Red China, but

Advance of the Coloured Peoples

scattered all over East Asia as well. Indian and Chinese women are very fertile: there are normally six to eight children in a family.

In the African tribes families have become so prolific that medical missionaries have been compelled to recommend the native women to use contraceptives. After bearing twelve or fourteen children, these women are simply worn out.

What effect has this extraordinarily high birth rate on the ratio of coloured people to white?

Let us take a particularly striking example from one of the African nations. In South Africa there are 15 million people, of whom three and a half million are white and eleven and a half coloured. The ratio of births is 1 to 40. The small community of Europeans in this land is being progressively overshadowed and encircled by the vastly greater birth rate of the Bantus.

This brings us to a further point which was made very clear by the "birth clock" at the World Congress. The world's population is growing eight or ten times more rapidly than the Christian Church. In Berlin it was plain for all to read. The non-Christian peoples are winning the birth race. The enormous fertility of the coloured, and so for the most part non-Christian women is causing the living spaces of Christians to be encircled, and making it into more and more of a ghetto.

Symptom 4 The biological ascendancy of non-Christians over the Christians is bringing about a progressive encirclement. What lies in the background? Certainly not just the fact that the highly civilized peoples of the West have lost their desire for children. No, the Evil One, who sits in the background at his controls, is planning to drive the Church of Christ into a ghetto, so that he can get his hands upon it more effectively.

2. *Ascendancy in Missionary Advance*

Not only Christians talk about missions and missionaries. So do other religions. We are living in a day when there is a sharp decline in Christian missionary impulse. The weariness of the older missionary societies is having its effect on whole mission fields. Some people are even getting up and expressing the opinion that the time for foreign missions is over.

This phase of weariness throws into still stronger relief the new activity of the non-Christian religions in spreading their doctrines and pressing forward. This new burst of life and change of outlook in the other religions is often accompanied by a hatred of Christians. In the religions of East Asia this is something entirely new, for Buddhism, Hinduism, and to some extent Shintoism have hitherto been marked by tolerance for other beliefs. The period of restraint is apparently drawing to a close.

After the last world war, a sect appeared in Japan which considers itself a reform movement of Nichiren Buddhism. It is called Soka Gakkai, and was founded by Tsunesaburo Magikuchi (1871—1944). In 1950 the adherents numbered several tens of thousands; today they run into millions. This sect tries to place its leaders in official positions in the state, so as to be able to influence politics. A notable characteristic of Soka Gakkai is its anti-Christian attitude: one of its aims is to expel all Christian missionaries from Japan. Japan for the Japanese! Away with the white tutelage!

Another sect in East Asia is the Amadya Moslems. When their founder died in 1908, he had half a million followers. Today there are 200 million. This sect trains missionaries, who go out into the whole world. They want to win back the areas which have been lost to Christianity. One interesting thing about them is that the weapons they use in their attack on Christianity are those forged by modernist theology. They say, "The best argument which the Christians had against us was the divine sonship of Jesus of Nazareth. This is now proved to have been a mistake. The Christians now have nothing over us; their Jesus is only another human being like our Mohammed." The zeal of these Amadya Moslems puts us Christians to shame. Here in the West they are building mosques, which are becoming mission centres.

These are the two most distinctive sects in East Asia. But besides these, one can observe a general revival of Buddhism. An astonishing missionary urge has overtaken its previously idle and conservative adherents. At Rangoon, in Burma, and at Colombo, in Ceylon, Buddhist mission centres have been established, with the aim of training and sending out missionaries all over the world. In the Buddhist ranks a determination to conquer is making itself felt. One of their best-known leaders, called Unu, has said, "The last war this earth sees will be a religious war. And there is no doubt about who will win it. The victory will be ours."

It is at once the tragedy and the shame of

Christianity, that it gives the impression of having exhausted its resources, while the non-Christian religions are evolving and pursuing plans for the conquest of the world.

Symptom 5   The new burst of activity among the non-Christian religions of the world does not merely mean a new phase of aggressiveness, directed against Christianity. It goes further than that. The forces opposed to the Church of Christ are concentrating their strength with a view to taking over the position held by Christianity in the world.

3. *The Flood of Occultism*

In the realm of things religious and occult, confusion grows from year to year. Christians who lead a healthy life of faith, based on the Bible, are rare. In the warm, damp atmosphere of a forest, toadstools shoot from the ground in no time at all. In the same way false teachings and demonic movements are multiplying in the dusky spiritual atmosphere of our day. From among the multitude of such movements, we can here only single out a few for closer attention.

Firstly, let us consider spiritism in various parts of the world.

In East Asia the cult of ancestor worship is practised by a thousand million people. This veneration of forefathers is not to be dismissed as just a sign of filial piety; as practised in everyday life, it amounts to communication with the dead.

Sacrifices are made, worship is offered to the ancestors. Whenever there is a decision to be made, they are consulted. As we have said already, this association with the dead is more than an expression of respect: it has religious import. It is a form of spiritism.

Three hundred million Africans are caught up in animism. This is the idea that in everything in nature there is an animate soul; and it has many religious forms. We find different conceptions of this idea, ranging from a kind of pantheism (where God becomes merged in nature, and Nature is God), to a general attribution of demonic existence to every aspect of life, both abstract and concrete. Animism, too, is basically a spiritistic phenomenon.

But anyone looking for perfect examples of classic and religious spiritism should study the religious history of Brazil. Here every form of spiritism is to be found. The ritual sacrifices of the criminal Macumba spiritists are still offered. The more intellectual Umbanda spiritism, which has become a religious cult, is also to be found. Most impressive of all is Kardec spiritism, which carries out extensive social work. Its adherents make great sacrifices in time, money and effort. They build schools, hospitals, hostels and conference centres. They care for the poor, the sick, the unemployed and the homeless. They regard Jesus as a great example, but not as the Son of God and Saviour of mankind. They show that human sympathy and understanding held in such high esteem by modernist theology.

This shows us that it is not necessary to be a Christian at all, to show human understanding. It is evident that modernist theology has become one "secular religion" among other, equally valid religions. The Bible, Christian faith and discipleship have, in modernist theology, lost their uniqueness. The example of Kardec spiritism makes this very obvious.

The whole public life of Brazil is dominated by spiritism as an intellectual and religious movement. The radio stations broadcast spiritist programmes. Newspapers and periodicals are edited by spiritists. In the army and the police force often only the spiritists are promoted. It is even said that 95 % of the doctors belong to a spiritist professional association. In one town it was stated by the Catholic and Protestant ministers that 90 % of the population were spiritists. Both denominations here pull together in a united effort to resist spiritism. But their efforts scarcely achieve anything.

In addition to such openly occult and demonic movements, there are abroad today others of a religious nature, which invade countries like epidemics of the soul. Men and women are gripped by these spiritual infections, and for a few months or years revel in the new experiences these movements offer them, until in the end they lose everything of inner, spiritual value which they had before. After the fires of the emotional experience have died down, they resemble burnt-out craters.

One striking example from among many: I know a female medical student in another country, whose father is a preacher. The girl experienced a sound conversion at the age of 16. For three years she followed her Lord Jesus faithfully. Then through the invitation of a friend, she got into a group of religious extremists. She caught the enthusiasm. The waves of emotion rolled high. For six months this

Dangers of the World

experience brought her satisfaction. Then the feelings began to wane. She lost her feelings of ecstasy, and in the meantime she had also lost her peace with God and the assurance of forgiveness. She was not simply sobered down, but utterly emptied and pumped out in her spiritual life. Through the ecstatic experiences, she had lost her assurance of being God's child. She sank into a life of sin.

Symptom 6   Occult and extremist movements offer people a substitute for genuine Christian discipleship. At the same time they are a smoke-screen of the Enemy of God, diverting our attention from his aims. In any case he is the one who profits, for all the time he is fishing in the dark waters and luring people into his power.

III. DANGERS TO THE WORLD

Our planet has become a small place. In politics, economics and the world of ideas, people are treading on one another's toes. Humanity is like an over-filled refugee camp. Everyone is jostling his neighbour. There is a struggle for space, a struggle for light, a struggle for water, a struggle for food supplies, a struggle for luxuries, a struggle for a little love and diversion! To these dangers within must be added the dangers from without. Let us name the most important of these.

1. Political Encirclement

Communist ideology is on the march all over the world. The approach of this wave of anti-Christian doctrine can be felt particularly strongly on the mission fields.

Worst hit of all has been the China Inland Mission. One wonders whether its founder, Dr. J. Hudson Taylor, who died in 1905 in Changsha (Hunan Province), would ever have been able to envisage that his work would fifty years later be destroyed. Faithfully and persistently he prayed for China's millions, as have hundreds of missionaries and tens of thousands of supporters since. And yet God has allowed Mao Tse-tung to succeed in sweeping foreign missionaries out of this land with an iron broom.

Other areas of East Asia have suffered a similar fate. In 1962 the Dutch had to evacuate West New Guinea. This was supported by the Americans in the UNO assembly. The part of the great island which the Dutch had evacuated was first of all administered by U. N. troops for one year. Then there was supposed to be a referendum on the question of whether the area should belong to Indonesia or not. The referendum was an utter farce. How could the primitive people of the inland region, some of them still cannibals, have the least idea what it was all about? The communist agents, on the other hand, who swayed the ignorant people, knew exactly what they were doing. The winner of the election was Sukarno. These political events also had their effect on missionary work. In Lae, the leading missionaries came together to discuss how the missionary work in the western part of

Dangers of the World

New Guinea could be continued. It is true that the latest political developments have rung down the curtain on Sukarno. But whether this means that the communist menace has been overcome for ever in Indonesia, no one knows.

I once had the opportunity of speaking to a politician in the U.S.A. He told me, "Asia will one day be lost to the free world. The hungry millions have no defence to put up against communist propaganda. One day we shall be glad perhaps if we can protect the north and south of our own continent from communist infiltration." This man may not be altogether wrong. Many countries in Asia are closing their doors to missionary work and the gospel: China, North Korea, Tibet, North Vietnam, Pakistan, Russia. Others will follow.

Africa and South America have also become outposts of communist agent activity. Everywhere there is the communist bacillus, which finds a good breeding-ground in people impoverished by hunger and want.

A really classic example was told me by a Swiss missionary. He has been working for years among the South American Indians in the Upper Andes. This missionary is an expert on political economics and agriculture, an unusually gifted man. He taught the poor population how they can better utilize and cultivate their ground. He laid out an irrigation system, introduced artificial fertilizers, and thus succeeded in increasing the yield fourfold. After this, the missionary introduced cattle-farming, bringing in Frisian and Swiss alpine cattle. Every family was given a cow. He showed the Indians how to make butter and cheese, and so within a few years raised the living standard of the native families. There was a decrease too in child mortality. The people had previously gone around in rags; now they began to dress properly.

So far, so good. Only one group was dissatisfied with all this: the communists. One day they visited the missionary and gave him an ultimatum:

"You must leave our country as soon as possible," they said. "We don't want people of your breed here."

"Why not?" asked the missionary, astonished. "I have only done good for your people. They can feed themselves better now. Hunger and misery have ceased. I have brought in cattle, and I am cultivating your land."

"That's just the trouble," said the communists; "when the living standards of these mountain people are raised, they are no longer open to what we teach them. We need hunger and misery, otherwise our party cannot survive."

The missionary whistled softly. So that was the problem! After a short pause he said,

"Thank you for being so frank with me. But you can't throw me out. As a Christian, it is my duty to do good and to help others. How could I abandon the people to hunger and misery? And the net result would be the advancement of world communism, helping it to achieve its goal!"

The communist leaders left nothing to be desired in the way of frankness. Without batting an eyelid they replied,

"Don't be surprised if something happens to you one of these days. On these steep mountain roads you will have an accident with your car or an unpleasant encounter. We advise you to leave the country at once, if you value your life."

Dangers of the World

Since then the missionary has been in great danger. Since the last edition of this book further information has been received, which I shall disclose, since it throws an interesting light on communist methods.

One evening a bomb exploded in front of the missionary's house. However, no one was hurt, but the wall of the house was split open. God had preserved His servant.

Another time they tried to throw a bomb into the missionary's bedroom at night. Again the attack was a failure. The bomb rebounded from a wire which was stretched in front of the window.

Now his persecutors hatched yet another plot. They fixed a bomb to the exhaust pipe of the missionary's car. Again the Lord held His hand over His messenger. For a fortnight the missionary drove around with his car in this perilous state, without the bomb exploding. How was this possible? The exhaust pipe had a hole in the front part, where the exhaust escaped, and the back part thus remained cold. And so the bomb did not ignite.

On the fourth occasion the communists attempted a direct assault. The missionary was overtaken by a truck on a steep mountain road. Suddenly the truck turned and stopped, blocking the road. The missionary was compelled to stop too. From the other vehicle emerged some men, armed with long machetes (Indian knives). As they approached, the missionary reached into his glove compartment and drew out a large army pistol. Seeing this weapon the communists beat a hasty retreat. The missionary said with a laugh, "The pistol wasn't loaded. It just served as a deterrent!"

This has given us a slight glimpse into communist

practices. Already two-thirds of the world's population is under communist domination or influence. The communists work with a resoluteness and confidence of victory beside which the zeal of Christians for their Lord's business pales into insignificance. What is the reason? What is their driving force? Is it just the goal of world revolution?

Symptom 7   Behind these temporal events there are other factors involved. The steady growth in influence of the communist ideology is intended to constrict that of the Christian message, and especially the Christian hope. Hidden in the background is a secret wire-puller, whose attacks are aimed at the work of Jesus Christ.

2. *The Hunger Catastrophe of the Last Days*

In the summer of 1966 about 2,000 dieticians gathered in Hamburg for a conference on the increasingly urgent problem of feeding mankind. It is estimated that every 40 years the human race doubles in size. On this calculation there will be some 7,000 million people to feed by the year 2000, and by 2040 something like 14,000 million.

This rapid growth in world population presents the dieticians with simply insoluble problems. Hundreds of possibilities were considered.

A Frenchman stated that the Sahara has plenty of water at a depth of 230 feet. Why not build an atomic-powered pump to bring this mass of water to the surface and so irrigate the desert? An

Dangers of the World

Australian drew attention to certain types of plants which require little nourishment, and are yet at the same time tough enough to be considered for planting in the desert. Especially suitable are the plants of the genus Chenopodae, which need little water and can store it for long periods, and in addition have a high nutritive value. Others again spoke of the possibility of laying a "foam-rubber" carpet of seeds and nutrients over the desert. The concentrated nutrients would enable the plants to grow, and they in their turn would serve to hold water and form humus. The production of fresh water from salt water was also discussed.

Another topic at the conference concerned the great jungle areas of the earth, which could be cultivated to feed mankind. One of our most important accessories to future cultivation of the earth will be atomic power. Giant ploughs and tractors powered by nuclear energy — fine ideas, if man were sensible enough to use this power solely for peaceful purposes. Up to now, however, 98 % of the world's nuclear power has been either used or reserved for military projects. Who is to bring about this sudden change in the heart of man, which will make him use the basic forces of creation no longer for destruction, but to give life? Isn't it just a piece of wishful thinking, incapable of fulfilment? Will these high hopes ever be realised before Christ comes again and sets up His millenial reign on earth? Then, in the words of the prophet Isaiah (ch. 2 v. 4),

> "He shall judge between the nations, and shall decide for many peoples; and they shall beat their swords into ploughshares, and their spears into pruning hooks; nation shall not

> lift up sword against nation, neither shall they
> learn war any more."

For all their plans and all their optimism, these experts on nutrition could not exorcise the spectre of starvation which is appearing on the horizon of the future. Indeed, there are today already a thousand million people and more, who never get enough for their daily needs. If this is so now, with a world population of 3,300 millions, what will it be like in 40 years' time, when there are twice as many mouths to feed?

Just how little we can allow ourselves to share the optimism of the World Economic Congress, the mention of a few alarming events will show.

Following the H-bomb tests of the U.S.A. in the Pacific, enormous numbers of fish were found to be contaminated by radiation. The fishing fleets of various nations working in the Pacific area caught radioactive tunnyfish for years afterwards.

Following the Russian H-bomb tests in Siberia, westerly winds swept radioactive clouds over to Alaska. The rain contaminated mosses and lichens of the northern tundra, and through them the Karibu, or wild reindeer, which feed on these plants. When the Americans tested the meat, they found to their alarm that the radioactivity had passed the danger level.

Both these reports show that up to now atomic energy has been responsible not for the opening up of new sources of food, but rather for the destruction of large existing reserves. This information is, of course, not widely publicized, for to do so might lead people to panic.

But the most striking evidence that the optimism of these 2,000 nutricians does not match up to the

Dangers of the World

facts of the case is afforded by starving India. If the "authorities" on the subject believe that they can one day feed 14,000 million people, they should begin by providing bread for the 100 million starving people in that country. If they cannot master the "little" task of the present, how can they expect us to believe them concerning the greater task of the future?

Are we not striding with extreme rapidity towards the time described in Revelation 6:5, 6?

> "And I saw, and behold, a black horse, and its rider had a balance in his hand; and I heard what seemed to be a voice in the midst of the four living creatures saying, 'A quart of wheat for a denarius and three quarts of barley for a denarius; but do not harm oil and wine!'"

A hunger catastrophe is looming on the horizon. Probably the non-white peoples will be the first to feel it, the West, with its riches and high living standards, the last. Therefore the white nations will be the object of the world's envy and embitterment. They will be accused of mismanagement, as well as of exploiting and endangering the other peoples.

Symptom 8   The watchword of this hunger catastrophe will be: "The whites have failed, it is the fault of the Christians! They are responsible for the starvation of the other nations!" And who stands behind this façade of famine? Not the unjust distribution of goods — no, the Evil One from the realm of darkness seeks, through his attacks on Christians, to defeat the Nazarene.

3. Radioactivity and the Fear of the Atom

An Italian politican allowed his life-story to be published anonymously by a psycho-therapist. The book, which was a literary success, was entitled, significantly, "I am afraid". A few years before his death Winston Churchill said, "The reins of world government have slipped from the hands of the great powers. They can no longer solve the problems which beset them."

It is not only in the political world that we meet this fear: it invades every sphere of life.

Let us take a quick look at the most marked form of fear: the fear of the atom, bound up as it is with the increase in radiation. Bernhard Philberth, in his well-known book "Christliche Prophetie und Nuklearenergie" (Christian prophecy and nuclear energy), speaks of the so-called "hot particles". What are these? Radioactive atomic nuclei condense in the course of an H-bomb explosion into tiny granules, with sizes in the order of 10^{-12}. When we breathe, the floating particles are drawn in with the air, and normally they are then expelled again. But once a year on an average, a hot particle stays in the lung and imbeds itself in the tissue. These hot particles lead to cancer. Philberth says that, if the worst comes to the worst, the whole human race could die of cancer in 30 years from now. We do not need to consider this possibility, however, for in the Bible, the book of Revelation knows of no such annihilation of mankind. Philberth believes, however, that even in the best circumstances hundreds of thousands of people will suffer from terrible cancerous ulcers. Here Philberth will be proved right. In Rev. 16:2 we are told, "... foul and evil sores came upon the men..."

Dangers of the World

Philberth is a nuclear physicist. It is therefore remarkable that his theories have the support of those engaged in cancer research. The latter claim, indeed, that 5 % of the human race is already infected with cancer.

There is another problem that arises in connection with the use of nuclear energy, which can only be touched on here. In the last fews years the U.S.A. has been making tests with the cobalt bomb. The results were so terrifying that the U.S.A. at first dissociated itself from the experiments. Measuring instruments for the cobalt test had been set up on an island in the Pacific. After the explosion the island had completely disappeared. The heat which was generated was also great enough to destroy the three ships which lay nearest the scene of the explosion. The iron parts melted. It was therefore impossible to evaluate most of the results of the test, for even the measuring instruments placed at a great distance were for the most part destroyed by the heat. A rough estimate placed the temperature generated by the explosion at more than 60 million degrees centigrade. By way of comparison, the temperature of the sun's nucleus is between 12 and 15 million degrees. In other words the heat generated in this explosion was about five times as high. We laymen ask quite innocently, "Where is this going to lead us?" And with that we move nearer to an understanding of 2 Peter 3:10, where we are told, "The heavens will pass away with a loud noise, and the elements will be dissolved with fire, and the earth and the works that are upon it will be burned up."

In view of these words of Scripture, the cobalt experiment is of prophetic and eschatological character.

We live in a time when prophecy is being fulfilled.

In this context we would do well to ponder something which the great scientist Einstein hinted at before his death. He told his friends that he had come across evidence of reactions which would release energy far greater even than that released by the fission and fusion of atoms. He had, however, determined to take his discovery with him into the grave. It was too great a responsibility for him.

We have, in these few paragraphs, only been able to touch on one of the problems of fear which beset thoughtful people. Fear has, however, many faces. People have fear of life, fear of crowds, fear of exams, fear of war, fear of death, fear of other people, fear of responsibility, fear of their own weakness, fear of an over-powering destiny, fear of the uncertain future, and so on.

The words of Luke 21:26 are beginning to be fulfilled, where we are told of a time when "men will faint with fear and with foreboding of what is coming on the world."

Symptom 9　People with insight are aware that there are mighty events looming. The terrifying discoveries of science in the realm of nuclear physics are creating the conditions for an overwhelming sense of doom to take possession of our souls. Fear has become the basic characteristic of our existence. Man is no longer master of the situation which he himself has created. The ship of humanity has lost its steering tackle, and another hand is trying to gain control.

4. The Breakdown of Mental Health in the White Race

Our age is marked by the call for the psychiatrist. A few years before his death, the well-known professor Viktor von Weizsäcker said, "West Germany has 4,000 psychiatrists too few." Today the shortage is still greater.

Successful psychiatrists are often booked for months in advance. On one occasion I wanted to send someone I knew to Dr. Alfons Mäder, a believing Christian psychiatrist in Zürich. The gifted doctor answered that his diary was booked up for a whole year in advance.

Some most alarming facts in the field of emotional and mental diseases were disclosed at a conference of psycho-therapists and psychiatrists held in Austria a few years ago.

A Swiss psychiatrist asserted that 4 % of all hospital patients are not organically but mentally ill. It should be observed that this figure did not include out-patients, but only those with beds in hospitals. The Austrian and German delegates stated that they reckoned with a proportion of 10 % in their hospitals. The highest figure was given by the English delegate, a professor at London University. He drew attention to the fact that in England 35 % of all hospital beds had to be reserved for people with nervous disorders. England has the highest percentage of depressives and neurotics in Europe.

In the U.S.A. the scene is even worse. An American psychiatrist reported that in the United States half of all the patients in hospitals have mental disorders. Among students, at least 30 % needed to be sent to a psychiatrist for counselling and treatment. Lastly there was the statement of the Canadian professor, who confirmed with a smile, "One Canadian in eighty has a mental kink!"

One of the facts discovered at this conference was that mental disorders are on the increase in the white race. The wearing down of nervous energy, the countless emotional strains, the "wave of depression" in the Western world, herald the collapse of the white man's mental powers of resistance. It is no wonder that in the field of mental therapeutics decisive measures need to be taken. In all the countries of the Western world the attempt is being made to develop a comprehensive system of mental hygiene, i.e. steps to protect mental health. Furthermore, a greater number of medical students will have to develope an interest in the field of psychiatry. The number of those specializing in nervous and mental disorders is not big enough to cope with the tidal wave of mental patients.

In the cities evangelists and Christian counsellors too are finding an increasing demand for their services from the mentally ill. During a week's campaign in Zurich, one evangelist had to counsel some 70 depressives. In a week in Stuttgart, about 50 people with nervous disorders came to see the evangelist.

What conclusions may we draw from this development?

Symptom 10 The tired nerves of modern man, and the wearing down of his mental powers, are indications that the Western world is on the decline. Mental storm-barriers are breaking. Day-to-day events are exceeding man's ability to master them. They threaten, grind down and destroy his mental powers of resistance. Without these, man is an easy prey for the impious forces which have already started their full-scale rebellion against God.

5. Natural Disasters

According to Matthew 24 and Luke 21, natural catastrophes are an essential feature of the Last Days: we read that sun and moon will lose their light; the powers of heaven will be shaken; plagues, famine and earthquakes will trouble the earth and mankind. For no area is excluded from the all-embracing plan of the Terrible One who is in rebellion against God. Everything which has emanated from God's hand, man and nature alike, is to come under fire. The ultimate goal of the satanic strategy is a final chaos.

Now that we are in the second half of our century, what stage have we reached in this rebellion against nature? A whole book could be written on this subject. Here I will mention just a few thoughts and some observations I have made personally.

In Puerto Mont I stood in front of a Protestant church which has already had to be built three times. Chile has often been afflicted by terrible earthquakes, which have not left even this house of God unscathed. The steeple of the last church swayed in the earthquake like a reed in the wind and then collapsed on the nave and demolished this place where God's Word is made known.

In Anchorage in Alaska a powerful impression was formed on my mind by traces of the last great earthquake there, which occurred on Good Friday, 1964. This quake was of strength 9, in other words even stronger than the famous San Francisco earthquake. The skyscrapers in the city centre collapsed; whole streets were pushed sideways. A tidal wave following the earthquake flooded great areas.

The seismologists (those who study earthquakes) tell us that in the last 400 years the number of earthquakes has shown a steady increase. It is even suggested that the earth's crust may have moved in relation to the core. This theory would account for the large number of disturbances.

Talking of movements of the earth, let us also at this point mention landslides. Some of us will certainly still remember the catastrophe at Longarone, in Italy. Here part of the mountain slid into the reservoir, producing a 300-foot tidal wave of water and mud. This rolled over the village and buried 4,000 people.

Natural disasters also include avalanches. A few years ago an avalanche obliterated several villages in the Upper Andes, in South America. In the last great avalanche in Switzerland, nearly a hundred people lost their lives.

We can scarcely relax any more. The newspapers are always reporting some new calamity — floods in the Po valley, giant floods in the Porto Alegre district of Brazil, and numerous other natural disasters.

One particularly tragic class of disasters is formed by the "dangerous girls" of the Pacific Ocean, between the Philippines, Taiwan (Formosa), Hong Kong, and South Japan. These are typhoons, which for some reason are known by girls' names. These storms race over wide areas, reaching speeds up to 250 m.p.h. We in the Western world can scarcely form any idea of the devastation and havoc which they cause.

In Hong Kong I saw the wrecks of some fishing boats, which a typhoon had carried several hundred yards inland. Near an island in the South Seas, I sighted a large ship which had been hurled on to a reef by the whirlwind. In Japan, there is often hardly time to repair the damage to the harbours before the next typhoon strikes, bringing fresh destruction.

Intensive research is being carried out into the cause of typhoons, but an explanation of their origin, and still more of their increasing frequency, has not yet been found. The Bible, on the other hand, knows an answer, for it reveals deeper underlying causes than any scientific explanation can show.

Symptom 11 The increasing number of natural disasters is part of the scenery of the Arch-enemy of God, who in his final struggle is using every means available for his work of destruction.

IV. THE BREAKING DOWN OF STANDARDS

The apostle Paul says in 1 Cor. 14:33, "God is not a God of confusion." When the people of Israel came out of Egypt, God gave them at Sinai their first great code of law. Laws are the first necessities, where men and peoples are to live together. Laws are protective bulwarks. Opposed to these laws is the devil — or diabolos, the one who throws into confusion. He works by sowing disorder; he needs chaos in order to win the fight. His efforts, particularly in these Last Days, are directed towards the breaking down of all law and order. At the present time he is having more success in his dark enterprise than ever before in the history of man. This gives us a gauge for measuring how near we are to the end of all things.

1. *The Break-up of Family Life*

In North America many parents have complained to me that the days when there was any kind of authority in their country seem to be on the way out. For some years a new ideal has been developing, which is called "self-realization". This ideal is shaping the education of children and young people. The theory is that, as he grows up, the young person should not be subjected constantly to authority, but have the right to develop freely in his own way. The practical outworking of these views produces some nasty results in home and school. Many of those responsible for educating children are no longer able to exercise a guiding and formative influence on them. Judges in juvenile courts are assisting the breakdown of all discipline by their far too lenient sentences. Children are terrorizing their parents, teachers, pastors and employers. They run riot, harrass their neighbours and pester the police. They simply turn their backs on law and order. This makes many see in "self-realization" nothing but the development of the animal instincts in man.

England, too, a country which in the past has often received new impulses from America, is once again following her great pace-maker. The British

Breaking Down of Standards

call their ideal of education "self-expression". According to this, a person should find the outward form for his life which corresponds to his inward nature.

And the results?

English teachers, especially those of the older generation, complain that they have no means of upholding order and discipline. It is not the teachers, but the pupils themselves, who have the last word. The same pattern can be seen in family life. The home is regarded merely as a filling-station and parking place. Fathers no longer find themselves able to forbid their 14-year-old daughters from sleeping out with their boyfriends. All they are allowed to do is to provide for their fifteen-year-old girl's baby when it comes along, since the sixteen-year-old father is unable to feed his offspring. A barrister told me that he frequently has to conduct lawsuits concerning the maintenance of children whose parents are 14 to 16 years old. In the best cases, both sets of grandparents are ready to help. This, however, seldom happens.

To put the blame on the young people alone for this development is, however, a fatal over-simplification.

Children often lack the security of the family, an atmosphere of love, as they grow up. The "warmth of the nest" which we so much prize is lacking. Young people have no one to look up to. When they fail, it is sometimes because their parents have failed. This break-up of family life is due to a whole complex of guilt, which includes both parents and children.

What interpretation are we to attach to these facts? The answer is given by Paul in 2 Timothy

3:1—2, "In the last days there will come times of stress. For men will be lovers of self, lovers of money, proud, arrogant, abusive, disobedient to parents, ungrateful, unholy." Here the apostle is naming the features of the Last Days. Today we are surrounded by them.

Symptom 12　Where the family disintegrates, the State and the whole world soon follow. And in the background the Evil One reaps his profit — though he remains unrecognised and his existence is denied.

2. *The Wave of Sex*

We live in an age which is pregnant with sex. The psychologists have a politer way of putting it, and say, "Our century is one of sexual enjoyment."

It is not our object here to present the reader with a collection of lurid stories which would only excite his imagination. We can only cautiously refer to some examples which may be taken as symptomatic of our time.

Genesis 19:1—8 records the particular sin of the inhabitants of Sodom. Paul repeats this record of Sodomite sin in Romans 1:27. And what is the present-day view of these sins of depravity? A Swiss marriage counsellor justifies homosexuality. When two Swiss pastors took the matter up against him, this marriage counsellor was covered up and protected by the Church.

In Gen. 19 and Rom. 1 these sins were the precursors of destruction. Is it different today? Have

Breaking Down of Standards 49

church leaders a right to invalidate the statements of Scripture?

The degeneration of humanity today has reached alarming proportions. An Australian believer who is a friend of mine made a visit to Cairo. Unintentionally he found himself in the midst of a tourist attraction. Before the eyes of the sightseers a sin was being committed which Exodus 22:19 puts under sentence of death. Scandalized, the Australian jumped up and ran out of the place in disgust.

Someone may say, "Well, they are Moslems. They have a different morality from Christians." Are there not things in Christian countries which cry out to heaven in the same way?

I was engaged in an evangelistic campaign in a European port. The minister of the church in which I was speaking told me, "In one school in the worst quarter of our town, nearly a third of the girls are either actually mothers or expecting before they leave."

An example from England. My informant is a Christian don in Manchester. When I was speaking at Manchester University, I stayed at his house. In the evening he drove me in his car to the so-called Heaven and Hell Club. We could not stop there, for the car would have been demolished. We could only drive a few times around the square. As we drove round, he told me that every night young people from 12 years old and upwards sleep together here. Sometimes there are 300 couples.

"Is there no law in England to protect the underaged?" I asked, astonished.

"Oh yes," he replied, "but it is not observed strictly enough. If anyone says anything against this, he is regarded as being old-fashioned and having 'continental' views. Young people who are still half children go around enjoying the night life under the eyes of the bobbies. They make love-nests for themselves in abandoned houses, and meet their boy friends and girl friends there."

We can close this horrible catalogue with mention of an incident which occurred in Germany. A Lutheran pastor in Hamburg was on his way to take his confirmation class. On entering the room where the class was held, he found all the confirmation candidates in the act of sexual intercourse. Children are confirmed in Germany at the age of 14, so all these young people were of that age. When he saw what was going on, the pastor nearly passed out. He wondered whether he could possibly confirm these young people.

We ask again — are we not once more in the days of Sodom, or of the fall of Rome? Disaster cannot be far away.

Symptom 13 In the history of the world, the breaking down of the sense of modesty has always heralded a downfall. Can it be otherwise today?

3. The Wave of Addiction

"Feelings by prescription" is a new slogan of our age. Medical science has developed psychodelics, which affect the emotions by changing the perceptual content of the brain.

This science is of course nothing new, for the primitive tribes of the earth have for thousands of years known plants which alter the conscious and subconscious states of man. In Mexico I came upon

Breaking Down of Standards

Indians who make a substance out of poisonous fungi which produces a state of intoxication. This class of plants includes among others the cactus Peyotl. From it is prepared a drink which causes glorious hallucinations. Mr. Zehnder, a missionary I met in Amazonia, showed me the Toe shrub, which causes the Indians who chew its leaves to fall into a dreamless sleep. Similarly, the Wongai in Australia, with whom I have also had contact, make a drink from a plant which removes a person's will-power. When someone has been treated with this extract, he is incapable of thinking for himself any more. He thinks only what he is told to think. The Wongai have in this way been practising brain-washing for centuries, long before the Russians and the Chinese discovered this method of enslaving people.

The only new thing in this science of psychodelics is the fact that psychiatry sees in it great possibilities for helping mental patients. An American doctor, Dr. Hoffer, provoked storms both of indignation and approval when he announced one day that a dose of 50 mg. of niacin, 6 times a day, could effect a cure of schizophrenia. This claim has still to be verified; but European doctors have also developed various groups of drugs which act as stimulants or sedatives. Phenothiacine, the Neuroleptica group and the Ataractica group or tranquillizers, are particularly worthy of mention. In the hand of the doctor, these so-called "emotional pain-killers" are of great benefit to the sick.

When, however, they are no longer used under the doctors' supervision, they constitute a great menace. It is to this that I shall now briefly refer.

Three times I have had the chance of travelling through Mexico and acquainting myself with the customs and vices of its people. A missionary arranged for me to visit a penitentiary for drug addicts and peddlers. As I went round, I kept seeing prisoners lying on the ground or crouching in a corner. They gave an impression of complete apathy.

"What's the matter with them?" I asked my companion.

"They are under the influence of drugs," he replied.

"How can that be?" I inquired.

"It's no problem," he explained, "the warders do a trade in heroin." So the situation is this. The prisoners are sent to the penitentiary because of their addiction or their peddling offences, but the officers responsible for carrying out the sentence are themselves dope-peddlers. They ought to be behind bars as well. But then who is to guard whom?

This illustration makes it clear that the Mexican government cannot control the drug traffic.

It is the same in the U.S.A. For several years a wave of addiction has been spreading over the country. LSD is a drug which is easy to produce. I have made many visits to the U.S.A., and have been told there that 30 % of the students and high-school pupils are in its power. I was set wondering what would happen if these young people, riddled with drug addiction, ever had to fight against healthy young Russians or Chinese? It doesn't bear thinking of!

The wave of addiction has reached England. Thousands of young people are ensnared. They run away from everyday reality into this sweet intoxication, and for a few hours forget all the troubles that surround them.

Breaking Down of Standards

But it is not stopping at Britain. It is a characteristic of such plagues that their influence today is invariably worldwide. Paris has whole groups of LSD disciples, and so have Berlin, Hamburg and Düsseldorf. The youth of the whole world is being infected.

Addiction is an escape into the subconscious. Switch off! Be free of your troubles for half a day! Is this a solution for the unmastered problems of life? No, it is simply a way of opting out of tasks which one thinks one cannot master.

Symptom 14 The new wave of addiction which is overrunning humanity today is a kind of chemical enslavement. And who is the slave-master?

4. The Breakthrough of Lawlessness

Stormy waves are flooding over and breaking through the storm-barriers. At the present time these barriers are at bursting point.

My missionary tours have twice taken me to Seattle, in North America. Two years ago the Beatles put on an evening of music and dancing in the biggest hall in this city. 14,000 came. After two hours of hot music, many of the young women and girls suddenly began taking their clothes off. A squad of 150 police did their best to fish out these strip-tease-happy lasses and get them into another room. There they had to stay until they cooled off. Only those fully dressed were allowed out again.

In the land of unlimited possibilities there are other sensations, too. During my evangelistic tour of California, my host told me of the bathing customs on the Pacific shore. In order to get brown all over, the girls sunbathe naked from the waist up. Their principle is, "If you can't take it, look the other way!"

A café owner was quick to see a chance of advertising his business. He hit on the idea of employing girls dressed in this fashion as waitresses. Shortly afterwards this alert businessman was prosecuted. The judge gave the sensational verdict, "There is nothing indecent in the naked breast of a woman." The defendant was acquitted. The ruling was reported in all the daily newspapers. It aroused the greatest interest. Other restaurant and bar proprietors began to say, "If that's the case, then we can use this method of advertising too." Within two or three weeks, there were about 200 places of refreshment in the district of Los Angeles with "topless" service.

No comment is necessary. Only the strongest stimulants have any effect today.

All these events cry out, nay scream out for the Lord to return.

Symptom 15　The one who is organizing this latter-day confusion aims at the destruction of man. Sex is to destroy his body. Addiction is to ruin his soul. Finally, the removal of feelings of modesty is designed to poison the spirit.

5. Indifference to Justice

I am no lawyer, and so I cannot approach this subject from a professional standpoint, but only with the understanding of a layman.

Breaking Down of Standards

During my evangelistic tour of Brazil, a manufacturer came to speak to me. His father had emigrated to Brazil from Germany, and through his own hard work and ability he had built up some large factories and so become wealthy. His son continued the work and made considerable extensions to his father's business.

His son is now in his mid-fifties. His two sons, the grandsons of the firm's founder, are pressing him to hand over the whole fortune to them now. This their father cannot bring himself to do, for up to the present they have made their name not as businessmen, but only as playboys.

Malicious quarrels ensued, in the course of which the two good-for-nothings gave their father a thorough beating up. So, in order to put a stop to the constant quarrelling, the manufacturer made over half his property to his two sons. This did not satisfy them. One evening the father was assaulted by the two rowdies and beaten with an iron bar until he lay there as if dead. Passers-by found the injured man, and had him taken to a hospital. The doctors — not the victim — filed a suit against the two sons. The one responsible was given a prison sentence of one year.

But if you think this playboy had to serve his prison sentence, you do not know the Brazilian penal system. The condemned man laid a bundle of banknotes on the prison governor's desk. This bought him his freedom. In the prison records he was noted as a convict, but in fact he was free.

Such incidents are not isolated. They are part and parcel of the general system of justice in South America.

After my return from Brazil, I told a top-level

lawyer in Germany some examples of this sort of thing. He said, "In 30 years there will be legal chaos in Germany too. The administration of justice is turning into an administration of injustice."

There is one area in particular where great indignation is constantly felt by the general population. Sex criminals, who commit bestial murders upon children, are often punished too leniently and set free again too soon. A butcher's lad, for instance, who had tortured seven children to death, got only 10 years in prison. A sex offender, who had been remanded in custody in the district of Brunswick, was released on the grounds of good behaviour. He went into Lower Saxony and there committed once more the crime for which he had been imprisoned.

The president of the German Society for the Protection of Children, Dr. W. Stille, who is a solicitor and notary, has stated, "The State has not done all it can to protect its citizens from the growing tide of crimes against life and limb." Dr. Stille demands the alteration of § 112 of the laws of criminal procedure. This paragraph states that a sex offender can only be kept in prison where there are "proven circumstances which can be regarded as constituting a danger that he will repeat the offence." That means that with a criminal of this type, one must first prove that he will relapse. Such evidence is well-nigh impossible to obtain. Not until he repeats the offence is the evidence provided — by the criminal himself. Dr. Stille says, "This loophole in the law is becoming a fatal menace to women and children." Experience shows that 50 % of sexual offenders repeat their crimes, whereas only 10 % of other criminals do.

Symptom 16 The undermining of justice will issue in the lawlessness of the Last Days. Jesus says (literally) in Matthew 24:12, "Lawlessness shall abound."

6. *The Abandoning of Biblical Standards and Church Ordinances*

We live in an age when all authority is being discarded. We have become a generation without respect: without respect for the faith of our fathers, without respect for the Bible. The well-known Swiss pastor Walter Lüthi once said in the Christuskirche in Mannheim, "If you take the needle out of a woman's knitting, you are left with a 'Wirrlete,' an inextricable tangle of threads." The needle in religious life — to take up the metaphor — is faith in Christ, or, if you like, respect for the Bible. If this drops out, chaos ensues. And so we have not only a chaos of justice, but also a chaos of faith.

This situation has been brought about by so-called modern theology. A theologian and sociologist from Marburg declared at a conference of the Protestant Academy in Tutzing,

"The sixth commandment, 'Thou shalt not commit adultery,' is a human interpretation of the word of God, designed for that era. Today, this commandment can be definitely dangerous to the commandment of love." In other words, the ten commandments were given for a former age; today they are out of date.

In case anyone should doubt the rightness of this conclusion, let me quote something said at the Kirchentag in Hannover (1967). The presiding dignitary of one of the German provincial churches was answering a question put to him by a girl about the morals of pre-marital intercourse. He said, "You don't have to wait for legal marriage to give you a carte blanche for physical love. That is not my own private opinion. It is the opinion of the church's governing body."

If church leaders give their sanction to free love, then psychiatrists have twice as much right to hold such views. True, they would not have needed to hold a Kirchentag, to invalidate the commandments of God.

When the Bible has been thrown out, the Church must expect similar treatment. If the Bible has become out-of-date, church attendance is meaningless.

This is confirmed by the facts. I was conducting a campaign at Lincoln in England. The city has four protestant churches. At the turn of the century, the churches were full on Sundays. Today the population is double what it was in 1900. But today one church is sufficient to hold all the churchgoers in the city. Church attendance is thus just one-eight what it was in 1900.

In April 1967 I was in Iceland. In Reykjavik a large Lutheran church is at present being built, behind the Leif Eriksen memorial, in memory of the great Icelandic missionary. I got into conversation with a Lutheran inhabitant of the island, and asked him about church attendance. I got the reply,

"There is no need for the building of this new church. The existing churches are not full on Sundays, but poorly attended."

After much questioning I elicited that Iceland has a church attendance of no more than 2% or 3%. Then why such a big new church? It is not memorials

Breaking Down of Standards

to our great past that we want! Magnificent edifices of stone have no value without living congregations.

But such drastic examples are not only to be found abroad. Let us take a look for a moment at my own country. A few years ago several pastors in Schleswig-Holstein applied to their church authorities for permission to discontinue confirmations. It was quite clear, they said, that as far as the young people were concerned, their confirmation was their last visit to church. The application was refused. Another group of pastors sent in a petition asking the authorities to declare Schleswig-Holstein a missionary area: the parish system should be discontinued, and missionaries sent in. This petition was, of course, unacceptable. It would have meant nothing less than the end of the National Church. And yet one day the National Church will have to come to an end. In the wave of persecution which the Last Days bring, such a structure cannot stand. Red China is a classic example.

Symptom 17   A blow has been struck at the foundations of Christianity. Behind it is the one who sits at his controls, planning out his strategy. The Bible is no longer the only standard, as it was for our reformation fathers. It is Satan's purpose to take the ground away from under the believer's feet. When, however, the biblical foundations are shaken, the structure of the National Church wobbles too.

V. THE GROWING STANDARDIZATION OF THOUGHT AND BEHAVIOUR

Traffic and news communications are today assuming global proportions. A person can board a fast air-liner in Frankfurt on an icy day in winter, and land 21 hours later on a hot summer's day in Sydney. Continents and seasons are thus bridged in a single day. One can even play a trick with the date: I myself once flew from Tokyo and arrived in Hawaii a day earlier according to the calendar.

In other fields, too, such developments are coming thick and fast. Through the medium of a television satellite, a New Zealander can watch a football match in London or New York. Thus a problem has been solved in the realm of telecommunications — or it will at least be solved within a few years — which interests our philosophers in a different way: the problem of synchronism, or "synchronicity" as Professor Jung used to call it.

This rapidity with which we can be "brought to the scene" will become a source of power in the hands of the Antichrist. Already striking signs of this development are to be seen.

1. *The Bombardment of the Unconscious by Mass Media*

The most important mass media of the present day are television, films, magazines and newspapers. Many of our contemporaries take in nothing else in the way of information. They are scarcely aware that they are thus being carried along by a current of "mass thinking".

Standardization of Thought & Behaviour   61

But much more serious than the unconscious uniformity, which these centralized sources of information produce, are the effects of subliminal impressions on the unconscious mind. In the last 70 years psychologists have discovered the significance of the unconscious. The names of Freud, Adler and Jung are particularly associated with this branch of science. The most disturbing thing their discoveries have brought to light is the fact that our actions are determined more by our unconscious than by our conscious mind. One of our best-known contemporary depth-psychologists has said, "We do not live, we are lived. We make no decisions; we are controlled by impulses from our unconscious."

The Americans, who have a very practical bent, saw in these facts a great advertising opportunity. In a film, which shows 24 pictures per second, they inserted advertisement slogans, one to every twenty-three normal pictures. The inserted frames were not consciously seen by the audience. Our eyes do not perceive something which lasts only one-twenty-fourth of a second. But strangely enough the slogan was perceived by the unconscious. Thus, on the one hand, the claim of the depth-psychologists about the dominance of the unconscious was vindicated, and on the other the sharp businessmen got their money's worth. Next day, the people who had seen the film bought the item which had been advertised, without knowing why they bought it. This method of advertising took on such proportions that the U. S. A. had to make a law against it. Business with the unconscious had developed into an insidious form of slavery.

The same thing which proved such a dangerous experiment from start to finish in the United States, is repeated daily in our slower-moving countries on the television screen. Quite ordinary people are prompted by programmes they watch to actions which, without the subconscious impressions created by the screen, they would not have taken. For we now know that our unconscious mind is influenced more than our conscious thinking by the programme presented to us.

Thus an old age pensioner, who had never committed a crime in his life, picked up a hammer after watching a crime film and struck his wife dead with it. At the trial he said that the feeling came over him as he was watching the film.

When the serial "The Red Scarf" appeared in New York, there was, according to the reports of criminologists, a rise in the flood of crime throughout the metropolis. Imitating scenes from the film, large numbers of teenage boys murdered their schoolmates.

Evidence of this kind is almost unlimited. Naturally it is never admitted by those who gain profits from these programmes: no one is concerned with deeper issues, when his money is at stake.

Under this heading of "Standardization of Thought and Behaviour" we can also include some items of research in the biological field. A few years ago a great sensation was caused, when an Italian biologist succeeded in artificially inseminating a woman's ovum and keeping the foetus alive outside the mother's body. For weeks the embryo lived in a nutrient fluid. Although there was great interest among scientists in this experiment, many Christians announced their misgivings as to whether such an experiment could be reconciled with the Bible. The scientist was probably interviewed by

Standardization of Thought & Behaviour

the Pope, for suddenly the experiment was broken off. Nonetheless this experiment, which has also been carried out by the Russians, shows the attraction that the dream of making man in the test-tube holds for biologists. As Christians we can view such experiments with nothing but the utmost repugnance.

Of no less significance are the experiments of a biologist at Freiburg University. He has succeeded in uncovering one of the special secrets of how human qualities are passed on. The bearers of heredity, the genes, can be influenced from without. This susceptibility to outside influence goes so far, that certain qualities of character in the foetus can be brought into prominence or emphasized. The tendency of these experiments is to make it possible to predetermine the character of a man according to specification or a carefully devised plan. These experiments are by no means to be consigned to the realm of fantasy, but give promise of great things to come.

Whether we as Christians should thus meddle with our Creator's handiwork, is another question. I would rather have children as God plans them than according to the biologist's blueprint.

Nonetheless this line of research opens up great possibilities for the future. A dictator will be able to plan people in advance just as he wills. There will be different types of man, which can be chosen out of a catalogue: the artistic type, the man of action, the beast of burden, the political type, the discoverer, etc.

Symptom 18 More and more opportunities await the coming Antichrist. By means of mass media, he will reach the depths of the human soul, and so get the whole man into his power. By influencing genes, this coming rebel against God will even have the possibility of creating a human race tailored to fit his impious designs.

2. *Standardization in Politics*

Dictators have the peculiarity of wishing to make the whole people over whom they rule conform to a certain pattern. One of the characteristics of the Last Days is that only he who has "the mark of the beast" will be allowed to exist.

My many trips to East Asia have introduced me to the method whereby the totalitarian régimes of the East try to bring about the political uniformity of their peoples.

Mao Tse-Tung has various methods. I have seen letters which believers have succeeded in smuggling out of the land behind the Bamboo Curtain. They tell of the unspeakable suffering and terrors of the people's communes. Young men have to work up to 18 hours a day on inadequate rations. Nor are the remaining six hours given over solely to sleep, for after 18 hours of work they are forced to attend "political schooling" for another half an hour.

Of course, not the whole of the Chinese population has to work to such a schedule. Mao's power is not equally great in all the provinces. There are provincial governors, particularly in the South, who don't care a straw for Mao. The huge empire is constantly being shaken by uprisings and revolts.

Standardization of Thought & Behaviour

Moreover, the 18-hour working day is only a punishment for Christians.

What is the object of such inhuman treatment? The physical and mental resistance of the young men is broken down by hunger and overwork. They are then ready to accept the political doctrines of their tormentors, something they would never do under normal circumstances. And so Mao achieves his goal.

But there are other methods too of standardizing political thought. In the larger cities of the northern provinces of China, huge loudspeakers are set up in the streets, which blare forth to the people a continuous stream of party propaganda. Passers-by are continuously bombarded with this terrible noise. They are blared at until they are simply tired and broken. If they enter a shop, the political loudspeaker is again to be heard. Woe betide the businessman who would dare to turn it off! Anyone who hopes to find a quiet corner in a café or restaurant will be disappointed. There too is the roaring sound-box, loud enough to shake the marrow out of one's bones and the fluid out of one's brain. No one can withstand this bombardment of noise. Mao has succeeded again.

Other experts in the field of political standardization are the Russians. Their methods are probably even more cleverly worked out than those of the Chinese. The Chinese make up for it in brutality.

Let us single out just one method, from the abundance of Bolshevist specialities. Here the victim for brainwashing and radical realignment of thought is locked in a sound-proof cell. This room is totally insulated from every kind of noise. So completely is every sound blocked off, that the victim can hear nothing but his own breathing. After several hours of this total silence the victim can even hear his own blood circulating. He hears the rushing of the blood through his arteries and the beating of his heart.

After two days of this treatment, the candidate for political realignment is near to madness. When he first hears the sound of a human voice again — uttering, of course, a political slogan — he finds in the sound a real relief. A person who has undergone this experience is never the same again.

The Russians have, however, made one miscalculation. This method does not invariably cause a state of intense emotional terror: it can, in certain circumstances, have two positive side-effects.

In this sound-proof cell, a person is completely alone with himself. He sees his past, his guilt, the futility of his life. He also feels his inability to escape from God.

The other positive effect of this process is that which Christians have experienced. Genuine followers of Jesus are the only people who can endure the soundless cell without suffering a great deal of harm. Even there the hand of Jesus reaches out to them. His promise holds good even in the re-education cell, that "none shall pluck them out of my hand."

It is a comforting prospect to know that, in all the approaching terrors of the Last Days, Jesus will not let His children slip out of His hand. He will bring us through.

Another thing which falls under this heading of "Standardization in Politics" is the idea of planning a single economic system for the whole world. Here we can gain much information out of a report from the work of the United Nations.

In a working sub-committee of the U. N. O. in Geneva, the delegate of a communist country put forward the following proposal. The U. N. O. should be abolished, and a "World Tribunal" set up in its place. This new judicial body should be made owner of the total wealth of mankind. All bank accounts and investments would be confiscated by this umbrella organization. Every person upon the earth would be given a number and a certain sum of money in a new international currency. The practice among rich people of living on independent means should cease forthwith, but so also should the payment of pensions to the disabled. "If anyone will not work, let him not eat." Everyone must be employed on production. Every time anything is bought or sold, the allocated number must be used. This new economic system should also be strengthened by an ideology: Church and State should be united to form one single organization. In this politically and economically united state, the individual must not be allowed to have any additional loyalties. He must toe the political and ideological party line. The biblical calendar system, as used up till now, should be altered, making Sunday the day set aside for remembering the foundation of this "magnificent new political and economic order". If anyone refuses to co-operate in this system, his number should be taken away, thus destroying his whole livelihood.

The origin of this social system is at once obvious. Various socialist radicals and reformers have taken a hand in producing it. But, to some extent, these ideas are already being put into practice in Red

China today. The free and liberal-minded nations will, of course, take the greatest care to prevent the introduction of such reforms as these; yet in the long run the West will not be able to hinder this development, because biblical prophecy has foreseen and foretold just such a situation at the end of the world.

Although the suggestions of this U. N. delegate fortunately still represent nothing more than a utopian dream, we shall one day be rudely surprised by their realization. For the prophecy of Revelation 13:16, 17 will be fulfilled,

"The beast causes all . . . to be marked on the right hand or the forehead, so that no one can buy or sell unless he has the mark, that is, the name of the beast or the number of its name."

From the viewpoint of this biblical prophecy that U. N. delegate is a prophet in spite of himself.

Symptom 19   The process of political and economic standardization, with all its satanic devices, is paving the way for the final kingdom of Antichrist. The tools are already being forged, with which the coming Antichrist will belabour mankind.

3. The Idea of Religious Unity

It is no coincidence that political thought is not alone in aiming at world revolution and world domination. Religious thinking is also tending in this direction. Today the urge for world power is to be seen on every hand. Let us illustrate this

Standardization of Thought & Behaviour

first of all in the case of a non-Christian religion, the "Bahai World Religion".

The founder of the Bahai religion is Bahaollah, who has appointed his son Abdul Baha as his administrator. The religion's name tells us at once that its adherents want to create a universal, united world religion. They want to found a law-abiding league of nations, with an international court of arbitration. Already the great, domed temples of Bahai are rising all over the world. The first one I saw was in Sydney, Australia; I have seen others in Haifa and Los Angeles. The ten principles, which are written up on these temples, are interesting and instructive. I am afraid I can only repeat them from memory in my own words, but they are based on the aim of producing a universal human culture, and the means for achieving this end are: a united world government, united world political policies, a united world economic system, a single language, a standard currency. The final goal is a united faith and united worship, which will include all religions.

I am not for a moment denying the good intentions of the Bahai. There is something attractive about this system. Between Christianity and Bahai, however, there is no bridge. Jesus says, "I am the way, I am the truth."

The thing about the Bahai principles which arrests our attention is the aim of bringing together the whole of mankind in politics, culture, language and religion. Is that not also the aim of the coming Antichrist?

In Christian circles similar efforts are being made towards unity. We refer to the ecumenical movement. This movement has been marked off in its 60-odd years' history by the world missionary conferences in Edinburgh (1910), Jerusalem (1928), Tambaram, Madras (1938), Whitby, Canada (1947). In 1948 the World Council of Churches was constituted in Amsterdam. Further full assemblies followed in 1954 at Evanston, near Chicago, in 1961 at New Delhi, and in 1963 at Montreal.

When we speak of the "Oecumene", we mean a movement aimed at uniting the churches. The affiliated member churches retain the freedom to form their own opinions. Earnest consultations are, however, held on the question of the degree of unity which can be reached between the churches. At the present time 214 churches belong to the World Council.

A detailed description of the Oecumene is not possible here. I would however recommend the clearly written assessment of the situation by my friend Dr. Bergmann, entitled "Oekumene, wohin gehst du?" (Schriftenmissionsverlag Gladbeck).

Here I have only room for some brief comments. The background to these comments is, however, formed by many separate observations I have made. Firstly, I have noticed that I can have fellowship and times of prayer with any true follower of Jesus who belongs to one of the member churches. Years ago I used to have daily prayer together with a believing Catholic priest. It is also to be welcomed that the individual Christian churches are making approaches to one another, seeking a human understanding of one another.

In practice, however, the Oecumene has another face. In the last ten years missionary travels have taken me to over 400 mission stations on all five continents. If I were to record all the complaints I have heard from Protestant missionaries about the counter-action of Catholic missionaries, the result would be a frightful catalogue of shocking religious aberrations. For example, let us take a very recent report from Yap, in the Pacific. For years Protestant missionaries have been working here. Suddenly a Catholic missionary has appeared, who has begun to cause the islanders to suspect his Protestant counterparts. The Catholic allows the islanders to continue all their heathen customs, and declares, "If you obey the Protestant missionaries, you will be visited by plagues and die."

In South America a Protestant missionary complained to me that his Catholic colleague had set up an enormous loudspeaker near to the Protestant mission station. This blared away from morn till late at night, racking the nerves of all the neighbours. Again and again the Protestant missionary asked that a stop might be put to the nuisance. In vain! The missionary had no other choice but to move. The "loudspeaker" had achieved the object for which it had been placed there. That is what Oecumene can look like in practice. I could add to the list from my own experience.

Much more important, though, than any example of unecumenical behaviour is the threat that a World Church will develop, and that the church will thus become a world power. To get the total picture, all the little stones of the mosaic must be pieced together. Is it not a sign of the times when, after centuries of division, the heads of the Roman Catholic and Greek Orthodox Churches — the inimical brothers — meet again? Is it not an indication, when Holland's Old Catholics have talks with Rome about reunion? Is it of no significance that the Anglican Archbishop of Canterbury, Dr. Ramsey, has made a visit to the Pope in Rome? It was another sign of this whole development when Professor W. Geiger, the president of the German Catholic Congress (the R. C. equivalent of the Protestant "Kirchentag"), made the suggestion that in a few years' time they should join this annual congress with the "Kirchentag". If these indications have not opened your eyes, listen to the following reports.

Mohammedans, Hindus, Buddhists and representatives of various Christian denominations joined together in a festival service in the Anglican church of St. Martin-in-the-Fields in London. This religious ceremony was an attempt to give a new form to a national festival, which in the future will perhaps be similarly celebrated throughout Great Britain. The service was broadcast on the television. It began with the singing of the National Anthem, then the Anglican Bishop of Kensington spoke a confession of faith, then an Indian read from the Hindu Gita, a Mohammedan sheikh from the Koran, and an orthodox Archimandrite from the Bible.

On July 2nd 1967, the following invitation was published in the Frankfurt newspaper "The North-West Courier",

> "The BAHAI temple near Langenhain, Taunus, is the destination of our outing on Sunday, 13th Aug. 1967 . . . We shall be taking part in the service from 3 p.m. to 3.30 p.m. Seats may be booked at the pastorate of the (Protestant) Church of the Resurrection, Frankfurt-Pfraunheim, Grabenstr. 2."

For the realization of a worldwide united religion, there could be no better combination than that of BAHAI with the Oecumene.

These events demonstrate forcibly that we are

already well on the way to the final World Church. Moreover it is becoming clear that this syncretism (i.e. mixing of religions) will be carried out under the auspices of the State. The idea of a national holiday with a "pan-religious" emphasis indicates the coming union of worldly and ecclesiastical power. The result will be a politico-religious united world system, similar to the Roman emperor-worship, which cost many Christians their lives. True, this development is not desired by the Oecumene, but at the same time this movement is paving the way and encouraging it.

Symptom 20   We have some notion of what this development of a World Church will lead to. The Church of Christ will again be driven into the catacombs, for she cannot join in this apostasy. The coming Antichrist will begin by making use of the World Church, to ensnare the religiously orientated masses. Once his power is established, he will destroy the tool he has in the World Church. We shall see then the fulfilment of Revelation 17.

VI. THE GROWING RADICALISM OF INTELLECTUAL MOVEMENTS

The age we live in has a tendency to "go off its head" in every sphere. Only superlatives, only excesses, only orgies, only ecstatic emotions, are still in demand. Anyone who does not join in this hue and cry, this cupidity and sensual abandon, is reckoned a conservative, behind-the-times, a backwoodsman, immature.

The same tendency can be seen in the intellectual realm. The philosophies and theologies of our day go to extremes. Everyone is trying to outdo the other by bold new discoveries. Whoever can spin the longest yarn and is best at lying wins the day. Why not say it like this, in such plain terms that it cannot be misunderstood? For is it not a lie of the tallest order to say, "God is dead"? The "wise of this world", who say these things, are at that very moment living on the patience and mercy of the One whom they declare to be dead.

From the multitudinous intellectual movements of the present day, let us select just three for consideration.

1. *Humanism*

The word "humanism" comes from the Latin "humanitas" and "humanus" ("humanity" and "human"). Humanism is a child of the Renaissance. A new ideal was laid down for living, derived from classical Greek culture. What the Greeks had called "kalokagatha" (the beautiful and good), became known by the humanists as "the nobility of man". They sought to achieve their ideal by means of higher education. Humanism began as a movement among scholars and has remained so through the centuries. One of its best known exponents was Erasmus of Rotterdam.

A special feature of humanism was its tolerance. It strove for a passionless, noble life, based on a high level of knowledge and education. Only once did humanism show an aggressive face, in con-

Growing Radicalism 75

nection with the "epistulae obscurorum virorum" (letters of obscure men), which appeared in 1515 and 1517. Otherwise adherents of humanism were completely tolerant of other views, and ready to coexist with Christianity.

This makes it all the more remarkable that in our own day humanism's tolerant attitude towards Christianity is disappearing. Again let us take a few examples, to illustrate this development.

Oxford University has a humanist group which is very strong in numbers. In 1965 there were 2,700 members. When John Stott, the chaplain to the Queen, led a mission to the students at Oxford, the humanists in the university became extremely active, — but only in a negative sense. All over the place they put up posters suggesting that only people of mediocre intellect would go to John Stott's meeting. They also organized groups of people to interrupt the meetings, and made unpleasant attacks on the speaker during discussions.

This is the equivalent on European soil to what we have already noticed going on in the Buddhist world of the East. It is surprising how spearheads of attack are confronting Christianity in every sphere and on every side. Are Jesus' disciples unaware of what this means?

In Germany, too, a new humanist movement among students and intellectuals is, significantly, gathering momentum. The Humanist Union, which aims to gain a footing in the German universities, has been formed. The direction in which this Union is tending can be seen from the subject discussed at a meeting in Heidelberg, in the autumn of 1966, which was addressed by a modernist theologian. The title announced on the posters was, "Jesus of

Nazareth's humanist understanding of God." Here the intellectual and religious platform of the new humanism is made plain.

We can also see from this that humanism is closely related to modernist theology. Both movements are concerned with the true nature of man. God is ultimately no more than the mythological expression of the sum total of the good qualities of man. The idea of God is no longer theocentric, but anthropocentric, i.e. determined no longer by the revelation of God, but by the reason of man.

Symptom 21　An essential feature of the development of the Antichrist's final kingdom is that no area may be omitted. Every sphere of life therefore — whether political, scientific or ethical in hue — must be rallied to the one objective: rejection of Jesus of Nazareth as Son of God. Tribute is paid gladly to Him as a great man — only the central fact, His Godhead, must go.

2. Neo-Rationalist Theology

Ever since there has been a Bible, and more especially since there has been a New Testament, battles have been fought over questions of Christian doctrine. It is one of the signs of the authenticity of the Word of God, that it has up to now withstood all the theologians' attacks upon it. A professor in Hamburg has this to say, "No other book in the literature of the world would have endured and outlived the drastic treatment to which this one has

Growing Radicalism

been subjected by its critics." Let us listen for a moment to some accounts of the destructive work of false teachers in the Early Church.

> "You have tested those who call themselves apostles but are not, and found them to be false" (Rev. 2:2).
> "I have this against you, that you tolerate the woman Jezebel, who calls herself a prophetess" (Rev. 2:20).
> "They say they are Jews and are not, but lie" (Rev. 3:9).

Apart from a few exceptions, the general tendency in the Letters to the Seven Churches is one of "Christian tolerance". This "human forbearance" on the part of the early Christians comes in for the censure of the exalted Lord, "I have this against you!"

The biblical position may be defined by the formula, "Love the man, but hate the false teaching." We can pray for the false teacher, that he may be saved. The heresies and perversions which he teaches, however, are to be resisted with the utmost plainness of speech and severity! True Christians set up no stakes to burn heretics: that has always been the business of devil-inspired extremists. "The weapons of our warfare are spiritual and not carnal," said the apostle.

Now we are ready to take a closer look at neo-rationalism.

a) We are not concerned here to give a detailed analysis and refutation. That would go beyond the scope of this book. Let us begin with one of the fundamental tenets of rationalism: *ratio hominis mensura omnium rerum est* (human reason is the measure of all things). The Reformation principle of our fathers, sola scriptura (Holy Scripture alone is the touchstone and standard of our faith and life), is thus waived in favour of human reason. It is not man who must bow to Scripture, but Scripture which must submit itself to human reason. This reversal of the Reformation message has brought disastrous consequences, the extent of which can only be touched upon here. Everything in Scripture of a supernatural or transcendent nature is struck out — i.e. all revelation, and everything which goes beyond the limits of sense-perception and of the realities which can be investigated by our reason. Whatever cannot be comprehended by reason, loses its binding force for modern man and is rejected as mythological. Thus it is the opinion of modernist theologians that the following articles of our creed can no longer be accepted: the divine Sonship of Jesus, the virgin birth, the substitutionary atonement, the descent into hell, the resurrection, the ascension, the second coming, the outpouring of the Holy Spirit, the forgiveness of sins, the resurrection of the body. These articles, they say, must be demythologized and interpreted existentially. In actual fact they are all struck out.

The radical and blasphemous way in which such deletions are made was illustrated in a discussion between Heinrich Kemner (a German evangelical) and a modernist. The theologian said to Kemner, "The Holy Spirit is for the people. For us, only critical, rational thought has validity."

This brings us to our first conclusion in our consideration of modern theology: the statements of the Bible are examined for their "rationality". Luther denounced human reason as a "whore". But here

Growing Radicalism

man has been made the measure of what is and is not valid. The revelatory character of the Bible disappears; everything revolves around man. This means that instead of theology we have anthropology: God Himself must bow to thinking man.

(b) The second, very cunning device used in the "existential" interpretation of Scripture is the throwing up of a smokescreen of biblical statements. Frequently the same vocabulary is used as in conservative theology. Even the pietistic "language of Canaan" is taken over. This covering up is very effective. Superficial hearers or readers do not notice the cloven hoof, for they think they are listening to familiar tones.

A classic example of this shift of emphasis was the lecture by Professor Käsemann at the Kirchentag in Hannover, 1967. He was speaking of the revolution brought about by the Cross. With ringing words he painted the crucifixion scene before our eyes. He quoted from Luther — for what is our reformer not held responsible! And what, in Käsemann's view, is the meaning of the Cross?

"On the cross," he said, "Jesus upholds and fulfils the first commandment. Nothing else takes place there. But there is nothing more that can take place."

"Nothing more?" we ask. Käsemann only knows of the law and nothing of the gospel. The cross involves more than the mere fulfilment of the first commandment. Luther knew more about it when he said, "... who hath redeemed, purchased and won me, lost and damned as I was, from all my sins, from death and from the power of the devil, not with gold or silver, but with his holy and precious blood, his guiltless suffering and death, that I might be his own."

Our modern theologians have developed only a symbolism of the cross, not a theology of the cross. They cut out God's action on the cross — and so remain in their sins. As far as the forgiveness of their sins is concerned, they have by their own effort cut off the branch on which they might have sat.

Let us now compare a few points in biblical and modern theology, so that ordinary Christians may be able to understand the differences.

Biblical doctrine	*Modernist reinterpretation*
The Cross	
Jesus died as Son of God in our stead. He bore our guilt. Isaiah 53	Jesus of Nazareth was only a man, not the Son of God. No one can take over our guilt. His death is a symbol of utter consistency, a sign of faithfulness. Here we see an ethical perfectionist going right to the end without compromise. He thus becomes our great example.
Forgiveness	
"In Jesus we have redemption through his blood, the forgiveness of our trespasses, according	"Forgiveness means accepting ourselves as we are" (Braun, in Bad Boll). According to the mo-

Growing Radicalism

to the riches of his grace." Ephesians 1:7	dernists, then, we absolve ourselves by accepting our own peculiarities of character.

The Resurrection

We believe in the physical resurrection of Jesus Christ. "If Christ is not risen, your faith is in vain." 1 Corinthians 15:17	Jesus of Nazareth did not rise again bodily. Christ comes alive in the Kerygma, that is, in the preaching of the Church. Thus he experiences the same sort of resurrection as does Goethe, when a teacher speaks about him to his grammar-school class. The New Testament's account of the resurrection is only of symbolic value.

The Ascension

We believe, as our fathers believed, in the ascension of Jesus into heaven.	The ascension of Jesus is, in the opinion of the modernists, a legend. One of them has said, "Jesus cannot have ascended into heaven. In 2,000 years he would not yet have reached the nearest fixed star."

The Second Coming

We believe in the bodily return of our Lord. "This Jesus will come in the same way as you saw him go into heaven." Acts 1:11	Jesus will not return personally. He returns only in our own lives, when we by our efforts achieve a compassion like that which he showed.

To outline clearly the false teachings of the modernists, many more comparisons would be needed. Anyone who is interested is recommended to read the short, but very penetrating, account by Dr. G. Schlichting of Bamberg, called "Dreimal 12 Thesen gegen den Modernismus in der Theologie".

(c) "You will know them by their fruits," said the Lord Jesus in His Sermon on the Mount. The practical results of modern theology are already to be seen in the Church at home, and on the mission field.

Our congregations are being starved of the Bible. There is no meat in the Church's preaching. Complaints are often made by believers about the church newspapers, which are edited by modernists. Here, too, stones are often given instead of bread.

The influence of modernism can also be seen when we come to the question of recruiting Christian workers. Modernist churches do not produce young people who apply for training at Bible Schools and Missionary Training Institutes, or as deaconesses. It would be easy to bring evidence of this fact. You can ask any student at a church or free-church training institution, where and when he received the impulse and the call to full-time service. It is an open secret: modernists make no impact. At

Growing Radicalism 83

most they have energy and a talent for organization. This is of course no wonder, for they have no spiritual life. A person who denies the existence of the Holy Spirit, and recognizes only the human intellect, cannot be filled with the Holy Spirit. That at any rate would seem a logical conclusion.

On the mission field this problem is even more acute. Missionary areas have no need for messengers of human understanding, but a great need for messengers of Christ. An Indian in a high position said to me, "What do you Christians really want? You don't need to come to India, if all you want to do is to build hospitals and schools. The Hindus can do that too."

Missionary training with the terms heaven and hell, devil and demons, conversion and filling with the Holy Spirit left out, runs dry after only a few months on the mission field.

In travelling through many mission fields I have been able to collect extensive information. One young man went with his childhood faith to a missionary seminary. There he came under the spell of modernism, and was sent, with his new ideas, out to the mission field. After a short while, the older missionaries sent him back with a report to the home council that they could not use this modernist. I learned this from one of the missionaries concerned, when I was in the Pacific area.

Another example I found in Nigeria. There I met a missionary who had come out to the field with a modernist training. For him there was no devil, no demons, no such thing as possession, only mental illness. In the area where he was working, there were many demon-possessed people. The ill-equipped missionary himself became a prey to these powers, and had to give up his work. For 18 months he displayed the same symptoms as the natives who were demon-possessed. Prayer groups were organized to intercede for him. After a year and a half he was free. Today he is cured of his modern theology. But, most important of all, his experience led him to find the Lord Jesus. Now he has spiritual authority as he serves his Lord on the field. He gave me permission to relate his experience.

Modern theology serves as a grave-digger for the Church of Christ, and for practical work in God's kingdom. There is a difference between social work, acts of charity, human understanding, on the one hand, and what I do for my brother out of gratitude for what Jesus has done for me, on the other. The roots and the basic motives are entirely different. Charity is practised also by the Kardec spiritists in Brazil. They build youth hostels, overnight accommodations, hospitals, schools, old people's homes, and call Jesus their great example — but not their Redeemer. There are many other movements which praise Jesus of Nazareth in the highest terms, but at the same time politely refuse Him the title of Son of God. Jesus neither needs nor desires our titles of honour; He wants our whole selves.

Modern theology is preparing the terrain for the Antichrist. That is no malicious slander, nor a bit of theological cantankerousness, it is simply putting things in line with the Bible. John says (1 John 4:3), "Every spirit which does not confess that Jesus Christ has come in the flesh is not of God. This is the spirit of antichrist..."

Symptom 22   It is no blind bigotry to say that modern theology is a harbinger of the final reign of Antichrist. The times we live in are so full of turmoil, and of such fatal significance, that we cannot afford to draw a veil over what is happening. Let everyone who loves the Saviour of the world avoid every kind of contamination with neo-rationalism. We owe the Church of our Lord these clear warnings, for she is in great danger from this new heresy and has already to some extent given in to the spirit of deception.

3. The New "Art"

After a certain concert a music-critic wrote a withering review of the evening's programme. The conductor did not let the criticism go unchallenged, but protested that the critic was a musical nobody: he couldn't play a single instrument, nor had he given any evidence of having a feel for music. The critic replied to this outburst by saying, "It is true that I can't lay eggs, but when I have one for my breakfast, I can tell whether it's good or bad." Perhaps I too may be allowed this "egg-test" in making a few comments on art.

(a) First of all, let us consider music.

I know that every age has its own form of musical expression. Probably Johann Sebastian Bach would compose different music if he were alive today, and yet he would still bear witness as ever to the salvation of God in Jesus Christ.

This brings us to our point. "That which worketh Christ" was the standard once set by Luther for our faith and thought. The motto of today's music is the converse of this: what works up modern man.

Having a desire to be still and to meditate, I went one day into a lovely old church in a university town, which I had known for years. I had received an invitation to a concert of modern church music. I sat in a pew, praying. As an introduction, the pastor read the Advent psalm, no. 24. Then a brilliant organist struck up a modern piece of music. I was amazed at his masterly control of the majestic instrument. By skilful use of the stops he conjured out of the organ sounds I had never heard in this church. Technically, the performance was simply magnificent. And the composition itself? Nothing but discords! A torture for the soul! An intolerable strain for the inward man! It did not draw one towards God, but rather pushed one out into despair, turmoil, inner emptiness. No answer was given to the searchings and questionings of modern man, only a presentation of the unsolved conflicts in the emotions of contemporary people! And I had given up my evening for this! It was the impression left on me by this music which led me to write this section of the book.

The dominant force in contemporary music is centrifugal. Bach's music is centripetal, i.e. it seeks and finds the centre, the living God. The melodic caricatures of the present day flee from the centre, they break up, they destroy, they take away harmony, instead of producing it. Indeed, some modern compositions reflect the whole idiocy of our godless age. One of the most horrible examples, which was broadcast on the North German radio, is a musical setting of the Song of Solomon by a modern composer. As I listened to the bawling, gasping and fizzing, the groans and the laughs, I felt as if someone had locked me in the security ward of an asylum.

(b) In the realm of sculpture, painting, and to some extent architecture, we find the same tendency to disintegration and the same basic discords as in the acoustic art. Again I do not speak as an expert, I only want to do the famous "egg-test". As with music, not everything, but a great deal nonetheless, has been distorted.

In the centre of Rotterdam there is a modern sculpture which grips the attention of anyone who looks at it. It is the representation of a man who, terrified by the falling bombs holds his hands heavenward in despair. In this case the sense of disharmony and hopelessness in the work is justified, and can be understood. It is impossible to look at this memorial, which was set up to mark the destruction of the city by the Germans, without being deeply moved.

However, as soon as sculpture degenerates into a disharmony and confusion of forms, which has happened a great deal today, the art loses its hidden centre and point of reference in God, and has reference only to man himself. It points to the breakdown of the human image, instead of pointing to Him who alone is able to help modern man. I stood once before a shoddy piece of art which made me seriously wonder: is that a bent bicycle, or a pair of lovers in a close embrace? It was a bronze statue in Brasilia, the new capital of Brazil.

The new art is especially provocative when its monstrous methods of representation are coupled with tendencies to exhibitionism and pornography. I will give three examples.

In Göttingen a statue was exhibited as an example of modern art, which depicted a pair of lovers engaged in sexual intercourse. The superintendent of the Protestant Church lodged a protest against this exhibit with the municipal authorities and with the public prosecutor. He was unsuccessful. The judges awarded the work of "art" the ascription "of artistic merit", and the complaint was rejected.

At the nation-wide horticultural show in Karlsruhe, seven cheap "works of art" were displayed. One of these was a representation of the female genital organs. Visitors to the show called this creation "female nether regions with water flush". Protests and letters were all to no avail. The gentlemen from the Art Society of Baden, who were responsible for the display, probably think that the visitors lack true artistic appreciation. I regard these seven "creations" as a cultural scandal, and as an insult to the millions who visited the show.

But it has been left to Stockholm to produce the foulest example of this type of art. At an exhibition there in the summer of 1966, a giant, 80 meter long figure was displayed, of a woman lying naked on the ground. The body of this female Colossus is an anatomical museum. Everyone marches through the vagina into the inside of the body. They see the uterus and the fallopian tubes, then the intestines, the stomach and all the great internal organs. In the giant's bosom is a Cola bar. The visitor can pass through as far as the brain, and then come back, leaving the body via the navel. This brings him out on the top of the stomach, whence he can view all the heights and declivities of female form and grace.

To what extent the Christian Church protested

Growing Radicalism

against this embodiment of bad taste and ugliness, I do not know. A quite excellent article about it was written by a journalist in the "Geistige Welt" newspaper on July 23rd, 1966. The article is concerned not only with this monster in Stockholm, but at the same time with the whole movement in art here symbolized. To quote,

"Plumbers, metal-workers and other artisans, scrap-merchants and rag-and-bone men, need no longer go short of their due honours in the cultural world. The door to the upper regions of the human race has been open to them, ever since it became known that rusty bicycle wheels, dented saucepans and old sparking-plugs are media eminently suited to the portrayal of the world we live in. Adjustable pliers, soldering irons and hammers are all you need, in order to bend and join together the refuse of today's affluent society, to form the emblems of the existential crisis which our contemporary artists give us by the ton. The plea for the dignity of man is made by portraits constructed out of dusters, touched up with Prussian blue and completed with a handbrush on top. Occasionally naked ladies are dipped in crimson dye and rolled over a canvas — a technique which produces a result giving the impression of an entirely new feeling for the nude. Descents into hell are made with the help of the vacuum cleaner; the end of the world masquerades as a faulty sparking-plug; and still lifes take place in the dustbin.

The unsurpassable of present-day artistic charlatanism adorns, however, the foyer of a Stockholm museum. There an oversized Venus reclines in an unmistakable posture, her interior, thanks to statistically faultless construction, open for the public to come and see. Visitors squeeze themselves in single file along the lower passage of the female Colossus and find, in the course of their lengthy walk through the various parts of the body ample opportunity for studying anatomical details...

The spectacle of this wonder-woman, offering to public view in a museum of modern art the secrets of her inward life, gives rise to a suspicion in one's mind. Perhaps her creators were not at all what one tends to assume at first sight — amateur modellers with a humorous disposition — but rather sculptural visionaries. This suspicion is changed to confident assurance, when obviously qualified art interpreters sensitively point out to the doubting philistine the metaphysical background of this monster statue...

Dazzled by cosmic insights of this nature, the contemporary art-lover who has up to now been fumbling in the dark, failing to recognize the power of modern artistic expression, hesitates no longer. He begins to uncover the deeper meaning of torch batteries, mouldy bread-crusts, and foot-cloths from the stores of the German army. For him even central heating pipes acquire a symbolic meaning, and a chimney fire takes on the character of a celebration of life. Rapturously he drinks in the aesthetic impulses emanating from bicycle chains gleaming with oil, and with an artist's pride he produces the dented mudguard of his two-, four- or six-cylinder motor, on which the uncertainty of our existence is traced out in interesting cracks."

This quite classic report represents the rebellion of sound common-sense against the senseless trivialities of a degenerating art — or rather, in this case, an already degenerate art.

Growing Radicalism

(c) And what of painting?

At an exhibition of modern art a rich patron once took the liberty of making a rather mischievous, yet pointed, joke. He put a paint brush full of paint into the hand of a chimpanzee. After he had demonstrated "painting technique" once or twice, the monkey imitated him. The animal splashed the canvas several times with the brush. The result was an "unusually powerful" expressionist work. That at least was the jury's verdict, and the chimpanzee's picture was given first prize.

Whether this story is true or apocryphal, I don't know. But it is typical. Even painting is today characterized by a disintegration of the forms we find in God's creation.

On my travels I saw a modern picture which had been awarded a prize by a jury. The artist's name had been kept secret. After the prizes had been awarded, it was discovered that the picture had been painted by a three-year-old child. No doubt the members of the prize committee have here discovered the "artist of the future", seeing that he has at the age of three already created such superlative works!

Somewhere else I was shown some drawings and paintings by mental patients. It is easy to get confused as one compares these with the products of modern artists, and not be at all clear who should be given the prize.

There is, of course, no rule without exceptions. I have seen other modern paintings which could not be reckoned as the result of "infantile or senile regression", but can definitely be described as art.

(d) And now one more glance, this time at architecture.

Here I want to single out just one category: church buildings. After a new church has been consecrated, the criticism is often heard, "The architect has no feeling for Christian fellowship." What is meant? Only a few architects are themselves believing Christians. How can an architect who is not a member of Christ's Church, and does not live from the Word of God, possibly design a building in keeping with the nature of Christian fellowship? So "parish centres" are built without any relation to the Centre of life. The people usually react to modern churches with pointed comments. One new one in Berlin is known by the citizens of this former capital of Germany as the "Lipstick and Powder Compact". Another church has acquired the nickname "Soul Gasometer". A church in Essen, in which I have myself conducted a campaign, is popularly known as the "Soul Silo". The church in Bad Dürrheim was called, after its completion, "The Soul Oven" by the local inhabitants. There is a church in Switzerland known as the "Soul's Ski Jump".

What have these developments in various branches of modern art to teach us? An English scientist and professor of architecture, who is an authority on this subject, has coined a phrase, "We suffer today", he says, "from artistic schizophrenia." It cannot be said more plainly than that. One of the main symptoms of schizophrenia is the inward split of the personality, the loss of the vital core, the loss of harmony. These, too, are the symptoms of modern art, and at the same time a reflection of our age. In order to avoid misunderstanding, I must point out that what I have said here has nothing to do with genuine art. I have respect for every artist who derives his gift from the grace of God.

Symptom 23 In many of the art movements of our day, centrifugal forces are stronger than centripetal ones. The disappearance of every kind of harmony shows that art, and with her mankind as a whole, is moving away from her Creator. And who will gain from this ever growing chaos? Nobody — except the One, whose first item of policy is to break up the harmony between the Creator and His creation.

VII. ISRAEL

Frederick the Great is said once to have put the question to his cabinet of ministers and generals, "Is there a tangible proof of the existence of God?" The answer came from one of those present, "The Jews, Your Majesty!"

Israel is the most striking of the signs of the times. Old prophecies are beginning to find fulfilment. The prophecy of Jeremiah (31:10), "He who scattered Israel will gather him", has become very topical in our own day.

It is a pity that a certain preacher in Berlin has written a book attacking Israel. This man must, however, have completely misinterpreted Romans 11, or he would never have been able to reach his remarkable conclusions. "The gifts and the calling of God are irrevocable", says the apostle Paul. That has a lot more weight than the private opinion of an expositor.

Israel is a miracle before our eyes, in fact a many-sided miracle.

The Miracle of Survival

From Abraham down to the present day — four thousand years in all — God has continued to have dealings with this people. Professor Karl Heim of Tübingen used to say, "This people has been reserved by God for a great future." In the course of human history, many peoples have risen and flourished, and then disappeared again, taking their civilizations with them. But Israel has remained.

The Miracle of Gathering

What did the prophets foretell? Isaiah 43:5, "I will bring your offspring from the east, and from the west I will gather you." Isaiah 56:8, ". . . the Lord God, who gathers the outcasts of Israel . . ." Jeremiah 23:3, "I will gather the remnant of my flock out of all the countries where I have driven them, and I will bring them back to their fold . . ." Jeremiah 29:14, ". . . I will restore your fortunes and gather you from all the nations and all the places where I have driven you."

These prophecies are being fulfilled in our day. True, only two million Jews have so far returned, and there are still several million among other peoples. But the process of gathering has begun.

The Miracle of Statehood

Since the Maccabean wars in the second century before Christ, Israel has had no political independence. In the summer of 1948, the hopes of two thousand years were fulfilled, when the State of Israel was founded.

The Geographical Miracle

Four thousand years ago, Canaan was a land "flowing with milk and honey". This proverbial fertility was lost. After the crucifixion of Jesus, the "early and latter rains" ceased. The land became covered in sand. This curse is beginning to come to an end. In the years 1901 and 1902, the early and latter rains began once more. In some places the underground water level rose by more than thirty feet. The ground can be cultivated once more. Corn is being sown; citrous plantations are growing up; desert areas are being afforested. The vegetation is having a favourable influence on the climate and rainfall. Geographers speak of a geographical miracle. The land is getting ready to support and feed a greater population.

The Economic Miracle

A young state needs economic foundations. In Israeli territory mineral resources are being opened up, especially those of the Dead Sea. In 1953 Xiel Federmann discovered oil deposits to the south of the Dead Sea, and shortly afterwards Professor Glueck found King Solomon's copper-mines. Great irrigation projects are being planned and put into operation.

The Miracle of Preservation

It is hard to grasp that, since its foundation, this little state has three times succeeded in keeping its end up against a force many times greater than its own. The peoples rage in vain when God protects His people.

One little episode may serve as an illustration.

In the spring of 1949, Israel was attacked by her Arab neighbours. The six months which had elapsed since the state's foundation had not given Israel enough time adequately to equip herself. Yet the Israelis won the day. In May heavy rain had fallen in the country to the east of the Jordan, something quite unusual at that time of year. Then the rumour spread that the rain was contaminated with radio-active fall-out from an Israeli atom bomb. At this the Arabs retreated. It was a miracle of preservation, like those reported time and again in the Bible: "The Lord thundered with a mighty voice . . . and they were routed before Israel" (1 Samuel 7:10).

In the second passage of arms, in 1956, the troops took five days to reach the Suez Canal, and there ended their victorious advance.

The third Israeli-Arab conflict was the 100 hour war. The Arabs had twenty-five times as much manpower as Israel. They also had three times as much equipment. Yet they were utterly routed.

We are not trying here to whip up enthusiasm for war. Wars are a sign of the fallen nature of our world. Wars bring immeasurable suffering to humanity. This was what attracted the world's attention, when it was made known that thousands of Egyptians were dying from lack of water in the desert.

And yet these military conflicts bear some affinity to the struggles of old: that of Egypt against the people of God, as they moved out of their land in about 1350 B.C.; or the struggles of the Syrians

Israel

against the northern kingdom about the time of Elisha, approximately 800 B.C. There is an element of duplication in the history of Israel.

The morning the war began between Israel and the Arabs, someone asked me,

"What do you think the outcome will be?"

"I can make no political forecast," I said. "I only know, on the basis of prophecy, that Israel will get the whole of Jerusalem and all the area to the west of the Jordan. God promised it to Abraham, Moses and other men of God in the Old Testament."

Four days later, these areas were in Israeli hands.

Again, it is in accordance with God's plan that the leading men of Bethlehem have already twice offered their town to Israel. At the time of going to press, this question has not yet been settled. But however it may come about, it is certain that Israel will receive Bethlehem also, because it belongs to the promised inheritance.

Even if Russia and the U. N. O. drive Israel back to her old frontiers, that is not the final decision. The time will come, when Israel is allowed permanently to possess the whole of Jerusalem, the whole of West Jordan, and Bethlehem.

Sadly we must add, on the authority of the predictive prophecies of the Bible, that Israel has not yet got her greatest battle behind her. That is still to come. One day a people from the North (Gog and Magog) will come and bring the most dire distress upon Israel. The Lord's hand will however decide the outcome of this last and most terrible of Israel's wars.

Are not these miracles of the last few months an eloquent sign of the times? He who has ears to hear, let him hear! He who has eyes to see, let him see! Israel is the most powerful indication that we have of the eschatological nature of our time. Our Lord Himself said,

"From the fig tree learn its lesson: as soon as its branch becomes tender and puts forth its leaves, you know that summer is near" (Matthew 24:32).

The fig tree Israel has begun to put down roots in the land promised and given to it by God. The tree is growing, the branches are getting sap, the leaves are coming. It is a fatal blindness which prevents us from recognizing the hand of God and His activity in present history, thus causing us to overlook a decisive sign of the times.

Two great miracles, or rather the two greatest miracles, of Israel's history are yet to come.

The Miracle of Israel's Conversion

Israel is still smitten with blindness. But one day God will open the eyes of the people, that they may recognize their Messiah, our Lord Jesus Christ. Jesus foretold this event (Matthew 23:37—39),

"O Jerusalem, Jerusalem, killing the prophets and stoning those who are sent to you! How often would I have gathered your children together as a hen gathers her brood under her wings, and you would not! Behold, your house is forsaken and desolate. For I tell you, you will not see me again, until you say, 'Blessed is he who comes in the name of the Lord.'"

The apostle Paul deals at length with the future of Israel, with her rejection and conversion, in the three chapters Romans 9—11,

"Lest you be wise in your own conceits, I want you to understand this mystery, brethren: a hardening has come upon part of Israel, until the full number of the Gentiles comes in, and so all Israel will be saved; as it is written, 'The Deliverer will come from Zion, he will banish ungodliness from Jacob'; 'and this will be my covenant with them when I take away their sins'" (Romans 11:25—27).

The Miracle of Israel's Mission

This will be the last great miracle in the history of this people. Israel will once more become a blessing to all nations. We may confidently expect that, in the millenium, Israel will receive from God the task of evangelizing the nations. Paul hints at this in Romans 11:15, when he writes,

"For if their rejection means the reconciliation of the world, what will their acceptance mean but life from the dead?" The whole argument of the eleventh chapter of the letter to the Romans seems to point towards the fact that Israel will once again take over a great task in the work for God's Kingdom here on earth. God carries His plans through. His promises, given to the patriarchs, have not been taken back. God's promises are more secure than the mountains of the earth.

When one considers God's dealings with Israel, one stands amazed at the faithfulness and mercy of the Lord, which is not invalidated through the unfaithfulness of His people. Terrible judgments indeed have befallen this people. By her disobedience and apostasy, she has brought the curse upon herself. But all the atrocities she has had to endure throughout world history serve ultimately the one purpose of leading her to the Messiah she once rejected. Through judgment and grace, God attains his goal.

"O the depth of the riches and wisdom and knowledge of God! How unsearchable are his judgments and how inscrutable his ways!" (Romans 11:33).

Symptom 24 God's purposes with Israel are nearing their consummation. The time of judgment on the people is coming to an end, though Israel has yet to pass through the final, terrible crises. This means that the last stage of human history before the return of Jesus Christ has begun. The Coming One stands at the threshold.

B. Drawing the Conclusions

The chapters and verses of the Bible which deal with prophecy give us no complete picture of what will happen in the Last Days. They do not provide us with any spiritual and eschatological chart, which we can easily follow. Nor is a timetable handed out to men, with all the necessary information on it. Paul, who was certainly a man of unusual spiritual insight, said in his first letter to the Corinthians (13:12), "We see in a mirror dimly." Some parts of the Bible, especially the last book, are so full of mysteries, that we must exercise the greatest restraint. So many obviously false interpretations already circulate among believers, that one cannot help asking when a new book on this subject appears: has the author drawn no wrong conclusions? When speaking about the Last Days, several guiding principles should be borne in mind.

1. There is no genuine spiritual enlightenment "outside the fold". What do I mean by that? That only people who have been born again through the grace of God develop a capacity to discern what is taking place in the spiritual world.

2. Only the Holy Spirit — not the human intellect — leads us into all the truth of Holy Writ.

3. Even believers must be humble enough not to attribute their own speculations to the Holy Spirit. Only to the humble, the contrite and the broken does God give grace.

In our attempt, therefore, to evaluate the events of our time, it is only in fear and trembling, in prayer and a spirit of enquiry, that we venture to seek out the footprints of God in history and the present age.

I. A WARNING AGAINST HASTY CONCLUSIONS

In 24 chapters we have explored the contemporary scene. Isolated details must never be magnified so as to lead to one-sided conclusions. We must be on our guard against misinterpretations. Let us begin therefore by considering a possible objection.

In the last few years various books have appeared which make much of the fact that we are approaching the end of the second millenium. Their arguments are worth pondering. But there is no lack of critics who raise the objection, "At the end of every century, people become thoughtful and start wondering what the next will bring; so much the more does the end of a millenium make people think that the world is coming to an end." Such criticisms contain a grain of truth. Anyone who knows his history will be aware that things like war, disasters, famines, plagues and political disturbances disquiet people and cause them to see current events in an apocalyptic light. I do not dispute the general validity of this observation; nor, further, would I deny that similar symptoms have already occurred in the past. There are in fact some interesting ways in which history repeats itself.

For instance, it can be pointed out that about every 800 years the West is threatened by hordes from the East. In 490 B.C. the Persians came as far as Greece. In A.D. 451 the Huns pushed forward to the West. In about 1200 the Mongol leader Djingis Khan built up by his conquests a mighty empire. No one could withstand his wild hordes of horsemen. This pattern would lead us to expect that in the 20th century the yellow hordes (Red

Warning Against Hasty Conclusions

China) would be a threat to the West. 40 years ago Oswald Spengler was already speaking of the "yellow menace".

And yet we must reject such a theory of history. If we use such coincidences of history to deduce a law, we fall prey to historical superstition. One example: In 1914 there was a world fair in Switzerland. After it the First World War broke out. In 1939 another great exhibition took place in Switzerland. Shortly afterwards, the Second World War broke out. When preparations were being made for yet another great exhibition in Switzerland in 1964, a prediction began to spread in fortune-telling circles that the Third World War would begin in that year. The evidence adduced was the interval of 25 years, and the three world fairs in Switzerland. World history does not follow such simple rules. If the Chinese are a threat to the West in the 20th century, then it is not because of the recurring interval of 800 years, but for the other reasons which we mentioned in Chapter 1.

What then of the 24 symptoms we have named? Is it purely a matter of history repeating itself? Not one of the items we have observed can be shown to have been so clearly defined at the end of the first millenium. In particular, there is nothing in the whole of the last 2,000 years to parallel the founding of the State of Israel.

We live in a unique period of history, without parallel in the previous history of mankind. The atomic physicist Bernhard Philberth calls it in his book "an age like none before it".

The Holy Scriptures say it even more clearly than Philberth. Romans 13:12 describes our era thus: "The night is far gone, the day is at hand." The time is getting nearer when the sun will rise on the return of Jesus Christ. But the darkest and coldest hour of the night comes just before the dawn. Is this hour not beginning already? The course of daily events has got further beyond our control than before. We no longer make the decisions: we are carried along. We are like those in a ship whose rudder has been smashed, and which has been abandoned to the raging of the storm. But what lies behind this situation, in which the whole world is involved?

II. THE GENERAL MOBILIZATION OF THE ENEMY

Winston Churchill was regarded as one of the ablest politicians of our generation. When he was still in office, he said once at a conference of foreign ministers, "The problems of world politics have got beyond our control. We can no longer master them." On another occasion he described the present situation with the remarkable utterance, "One has the feeling today, that not only the whole human race, but also the entire spirit-world, is in a state of turmoil." Note this mention of the spirit world. Churchill was not noted for his Christian beliefs, but this statement is of biblical or eschatological character. Paul wrote in Ephesians 6:12, "We are not contending against flesh and blood, but . . . against the spiritual hosts of wickedness in the heavenly places." It is a task of supreme importance for us to throw light on this fact.

In order to assess what the hour demands, we must once more take a look at the 24 symptoms.

General Mobilization of the Enemy

In the cosmic scene of the Last Days, clear lines of demarcation are being drawn.

1. The earth itself, which proceeded from the creative hand of God, is a target of attack. The terrible rebel, the prince of darkness, knows that one day a new earth will be created. He is expending his wrath on the old earth, which he has hitherto regarded as his possession. The increase in the number of natural disasters (Symptom 11) will lead into his hell-dance against the creation of God. In this connection the words of our nuclear physicists take on a special significance. Oppenheimer said, "We have been doing the devil's business." And Professor Hahn has said, "The H-bombs at present held in reserve would be sufficient to turn our earth into a lifeless planet."

2. Of all the peoples, the white races are the object of Satan's greatest interest. The sons of Japheth have become the bearers of the Christian mission to the world. The West is regarded as the seat of Christianity. The annihilation of the white man (Symptoms 1—7) is therefore one of the chief concerns of the prince of darkness. Developments like a race without living-space, a people without increase, abstract intellectualism without any impact, encirclement in every sphere, are all indications that Satan is gaining ground decisively.

3. Storm barriers must be broken down, if the Diabolos, the one who sows confusion, is to achieve his goal. The foundations of Holy Scripture must be shattered (Symptoms 23, 17), the traditions of the Church must be smashed (Symptom 17), and order in family and state must disintegrate (Symptoms 12, 16).

4. Not last on the devil's list for destruction

comes man, the creation of God's own hand. It was for man's sake that the Son of God came to the earth. Satan hates the Nazarene and His work of salvation. "The kingdoms of the world belong to me! I am the one whom earth-bound mortals worship" — so Lucifer would like to triumph: yet he will have to hand over his power to the Son of God. His wrath is therefore directed against all for whom the cross of Calvary is a sign of salvation. He is playing out his trumps. His strategies are aimed at the destruction of spirit, soul and body (Symptoms 13—15).

5. The Arch-enemy is seeking to inspire his subjects by unleashing a war on every front. Everything is made use of for the attainment of his ends (Symptoms 20—23). Spearheads are being pushed forward on the cultural front, the political front, the religious front. In our day he fancies himself near to success.

6. Most obvious of all the Arch-enemy's designs at present is his desire to wipe out Israel. The Arabs have openly declared their final aim to be the annihilation of this State. In making such plans, they are clearly doing the work of Satan, who is angered by God's election of Israel thousands of years ago.

All these developments, indicating as they do the build-up of positions of power by Satan, can be reduced to the one formula:

The general mobilization of Satan.

The powers of darkness have arrayed themselves for the final conflict. The armies of hell and the demon world are equipping themselves for the final thrust. Every aspect of human life is involved. We are constantly under fire. The great watchword of this last conflict is:

> War on the Nazarene!
> War on the saints!

Lucifer regards our planet as his property. When he fell away from God, he tore the earth and man with him. But since the cross has been set up on this earth, he knows that his dominion has been taken over by another, the Son of God. Now he is challenging the Nazarene to the decisive battle. In this final conflict the chief centre of operations will be the earth. We are already experiencing the preliminary skirmishes. In our day we are already witnessing the forward march of the powers of Antichrist.

III. HOW DOES THE WORLD REACT TO ESCHATOLOGICAL EVENTS?

When, after the resurrection, the women returned to the city of Jerusalem from the empty tomb, they told the disciples of this and of the appearance of the angels. At first the disciples were unable to grasp what they heard. In Luke 24:11 it says, "These words seemed to them an idle tale." Today the same mood prevails: tales, nothing but fairy-tales!

Let us follow this line of unbelief for a moment.

1. Firstly, a word about the contemporaries of Noah. The people of Noah's time had more pressing concerns than to listen to old men's fables. "He's got a screw or two missing," mocked some. "It's just a matter of hallucinations brought on by senility," laughed others.

In the meantime they went about their normal business. The evangelist Matthew records (24:38, 39), "For as in those days before the flood they were eating and drinking, marrying and giving in marriage . . . and they did not know until the flood came and swept them all away, so will be the coming of the Son of man."

They took no notice!

Humanity is just as hard to shake today as it was then. An example.

In February 1962, a mighty tidal wave broke through the dyke between the North Sea and the mouth of the Elbe. Several hundred people lost their lives. The outcome would not have been so tragic if those who were sound asleep at the time had heeded the warnings. When the flood was reported, the police sent loudspeaker vans into the danger areas in order to wake up the sleeping population. They paid no attention to the warning. A pastor in the same emergency area went round his parish from house to house, trying to wake up his parishioners. They did not take it seriously. When the floods lapped over the doorsteps and rapidly filled the ground floor, it was already too late for many. Can we expect it to be any different when Jesus returns?

2. Let us move on to the time of Lot. When the angels of God came and informed Lot of the impending judgment on the city of Sodom, he told his sons-in-law. "Up, get out of this place," he said, "for the Lord is about to destroy the city" (Gen. 19:14).

"But he seemed . . . to be jesting." Thus in the days of old did the men of Sodom shake off every warning. Their laughter sealed their fate.

How Does the World React?

Once more we live in such a time. In the course of a discussion between Professor Rohrbach (Professor of Mathematics in Mainz and a well-known Christian) and an adherent of the neo-rationalist theology, the theologian asked the scientist, "Professor, you are a mathematician. If Jesus really did ascend into heaven 1900 years ago, which fixed star has he reached by now?" For both Professor Rohrbach and the audience, this remark was simply blasphemy. "He seemed to be jesting!"

3. The prophet Isaiah, too, has a message for us. To the complacent people of his time, he declared (32:10), "In little more than a year you will shudder, you complacent ones." Has this complacency grown any less marked in our own day?

A little incident which occurred in Frankfurt will serve to illustrate the situation. It became a popular talking-point there in the spring of 1967. A drunk had kipped down for the night in a giant dustbin outside the main railway station. The next morning the dustmen came and picked up the bin. The man did not wake up. He even remained asleep while the dustbin was being tipped out on to the huge silo of a rubbish disposal plant in the north of the city. From there he was put on to a conveyor belt, which transports the refuse directly into the furnace. The man was still asleep, though by this time he was only a few yards away from the fiery entrance to the furnace. There he was discovered by a workman whose job it was to remove incombustible objects from the conveyor belt. Thus the heavy sleeper was saved just before a ghastly death by burning. The fellow got quite a shock when he awoke and realised the danger he had been in.

"You will shudder, you complacent ones!"

4. A further situation of this sort is found in Luke 19:42. Jesus is standing before the gates of Jerusalem and complains, "Would that even today you knew the things that make for peace! But now they are hid from your eyes."

For thousands of years the coming of the Messiah has been predicted. The great moment has come. The time is fulfilled. The old prophecies meet each other and intersect. Not only the people of the city are blind, but even the priests in the temple, the experts in the Scriptures, the guardians of the holy traditions. And yet,

"it is hid from their eyes."

Have times changed? No, the tragedy repeats itself! The prophecies of the New Testament are nearing the point of intersection. The signs of the times speak an incredibly distinct language. And those who should be concerned make nothing of these events.

A theologian, who has often travelled in Palestine and knows the situation there well, says, "What is happening in Israel is only of a political nature, and has absolutely no relation to eschatology." I am amazed at his short-sightedness.

I was once giving a lecture on eschatology in the Thomashof in Baden. The audience consisted of pastors, curates, and a few theological students, from the province of Baden. Also present at the lecture was a Professor of Theology. When I had finished speaking, he dismissed me with the comment, "You paint everything black and white."

How Does the World React?

Would not the words of Bezzel, if slightly modified, be applicable here? — "The world is bedevilled in the same proportion as it appears to be 'de-devilled' to the theological intellect." Bezzel died in 1917, but he foresaw like a prophet of God the growing theological darkness of our century. I am looking forward to hearing what he has to say to us in 1970, when he speaks to us from his grave. Before he died, Bezzel had a message sealed up, with instruction that it was not to be opened until 1970. He was of the opinion that by 1970 the Protestant Church in Germany would have gone out of business. The observations we have made in this book go to confirm Bezzel's opinion.

Jesus testified of the theologians of His day that they were blind leaders of the blind. What would He have to say today? In order to avoid any misunderstanding, it must be said that today there are still some theologians who belong to the Church of Christ. But they have become few and far between.

In Jesus' time it was not the theologians and the temple priests who recognized the Son of God, but the simple people of the land. Is it otherwise today?

5. The apostle Paul must also be allowed his say. In 1 Thess. 5:3 he writes, "When people say, 'There is peace and security,' then sudden destruction will come upon them." Catastrophes usually have such terrible outcomes because the people involved are completely unsuspecting and unconcerned. When the Babylonians were threatening Jerusalem, the false prophets proclaimed peace — and disaster was just round the corner.

Is it not the same in our experience today? One of our modern Bible experts has declared, "The world around Jesus, His disciples and the primitive church in Jerusalem, lived in the close expectation of their Lord's return. They were all mistaken. And today again people are mistaken who so confidently look for the Parousia (Return of the Lord)." So we hear once more,

"There is peace and security."

The answer remains true, "Do not be deceived; God is not mocked."

6. Not only the world, i.e. the godless and the "religious" world, will be surprised by the Coming of the Lord. Lazy and lukewarm Christians will be caught off their guard. In the parable of the ten virgins (Matt 25:5), we are told, "As the bridegroom was delayed, they all slumbered and slept." Waiting makes tired. Tiredness diminishes our readiness. Keeping watch in vain leads to criticism and doubt.

Are we not living in an age such as this? Many theologians are explaining away the Second Coming. The magazine "Der Spiegel" has spoken of the orthodox mysticism of those who still expect this event. The neo-rationalist theologians make the Second Coming an immanent event. They say there is no real, personal return of Jesus. When a person is set aflame with love for his neighbour by the example of Jesus, Jesus becomes alive again for him in his deeds of mercy. Thus the redemptive fact of the Second Coming is transposed into the sphere of our own actions. The breakthrough to a sense of social responsibility, to acts of charity, means the return of Jesus in our own age and in our life. Are these anything more than the spineless misinterpretations of unbelief?

It is a gloomy set of texts which stand out from Scripture as a comment in this connection on the events of our time.

> Tales, nothing but fairy-tales!
> They took no notice!
> He seemed to be jesting!
> You will shudder, you complacent ones!
> It is hid from your eyes!
> There is peace and security!
> They all slumbered and slept!

This tune ends in a very modern fashion — extremely modern, namely in a terrible discord. In Rev. 6:15 the other side of this blindness and complacency is shown,

"The kings of the earth and the great men and the generals and the rich and the strong, and everyone, slave and free, hid in the caves and among the rocks of the mountains, calling to the mountains and rocks, 'Fall on us and hide us from the face of him who is seated on the throne, and from the wrath of the Lamb.'"

"God has fixed a day on which he will judge the world in righteousness by a man whom he has appointed" (Acts 17:31).

Day X is approaching, inexorably, inevitably.

IV. HOW WILL CHRIST'S CHURCH SURVIVE THE TURMOIL OF THE LAST DAYS?

When we consider the world situation, we find ourselves wondering anxiously, "Is the Church equipped for the tumultuous days ahead? How will it survive what is in store for it?" This question suggests three perspectives.

1. In Luke 21:28 the Lord Jesus gives, in view of the general mobilization of the kingdom of darkness, the following instructions, "When these things begin to take place, look up and raise your heads, because your redemption is drawing near." When the terrible adversary has cut off every way of escape for the Church of Christ when the total blockade is in operation, there is still one way out — upwards! "Lift up your heads!" says the Lord.

Today those who distort the meaning of Scripture are denying the existence of the transcendent. There are indeed even some neo-rationalists who say, "The terms heaven and hell must be deleted from the Church's vocabulary."

This higher world, whose existence is questioned, is the place of refuge for the Church of Christ.

In all the chaotic developments and afflictions of the Last Days, the Church of Christ has one great centre of orientation: the vision of the coming Lord.

We therefore have no ground for a pessimistic outlook, anticipating only disaster. For us the question of prime importance is not a future atomic war, or fear of racial conflict or of China. We do not focus our attention on the looming problems of world starvation and increased radiation: our outlook is raised to a higher level — He comes!

> Lo! He comes with clouds descending,
> Once for favoured sinners slain;
> Thousand thousand saints attending
> Swell the triumph of His train.

> Hallelujah! Hallelujah!
> Christ appears on earth to reign.

2. But as Christians we also belong to this world. I should feel it was almost an injustice to our "brethren without", if they had to savour all the suffering of this earth while we walked in the "Elysian fields" of our faith. Do not let us forget that all men stand first and foremost in the solidarity of sin. Before we look for sin in others, we are first to see it in ourselves. The fundamental difference is only this: that the others do not see their sin, and remain in it, while the disciples of Jesus know about their guilt, but have experienced forgiveness through the grace of God.

The solidarity of sin involves also a solidarity of suffering and death. The Christian, too, experiences trials, sickness, and physical death. Again the only difference is, that we know about Jesus' victory over the suffering of the world, while on the other side the best one can do is to face it heroically. "One must just resign oneself to the inevitable." That was a Stoic principle, and is also a guiding precept for the nihilists of our century. The Christian has, however, another answer and solution to the problem.

The purpose of this brief section of our book is to make it clear that we do not believe in any cheap "Hallelujah Christianity". There is no sentimental maxim more questionable than the song, "Always happy, always happy, sunshine every day." The Christian does not only walk along sunny paths to his eternal home. If you have any doubt about that, let me remind you of a few facts.

What a struggle, what shocking persecutions the

Chinese Christians at present have to endure! In the Canton province, Christians who have been denounced are buried alive. Overburdened with suffering, is there any limit to what these children of God have to go through?

When former Communists are converted and turn away from Mao, they are cruelly tortured to death. Is that perhaps a highway of happiness?

Nor let us forget our missionaries. A few years ago, a missionary visited the wild Moro Indians in Paraguay. He was hit by an arrow. He was able to get to his car, and drove, seriously wounded, another 200 kilometers, before he could get to a doctor. During the operation, he died.

In April 1964, a missionary was again pinned to the ground with spears by the Auca Indians.

If missionary work already demands sacrifices like this, are believers likely to come through the most terrible persecutions of Christians, which are still before us, unscathed?

Have we forgotten what our Lord said (Matthew 24:24)? "For then there will be great tribulation, such as has not been from the beginning of the world until now, no, and never will be. And if those days had not been shortened, no human being would be saved; but for the sake of the elect those days will be shortened."

This text speaks unmistakably of the sufferings of the Last Days. Of course, this immediately raises the question among believers, "Must we endure all the last, terrible climaxes of the final sufferings?" I shall not deal with this question here, for I have already done so in my book "Our life after death". There are three possible answers to this question. Some say that the rapture (1 Thess. 4:15—17) will

How Will Christ's Church Survive?   117

happen before the great tribulation. Others place the rapture at the end. A great number of evangelical Bible students say, "The rapture is in the middle of the last week of years of the world. Not until the believers, with their prayer power, have disappeared, will the prince of this world have a completely free hand."

One thing is clear: we are already experiencing the beginning of eschatological persecution. The Christians in Red China are in it already. We shall not be spared anxiety, for as the Lord said (John 16:33), "In the world you have tribulation; but be of good cheer, I have overcome the world."

3. This brings us to our third perspective. As children of this world, we remain, humanly, children of fear. But at the same time we know of a victory over the problem of fear — Jesus, who said, "No one shall snatch them out of my hand" (John 10:28).

After the second World War, people were deeply moved by a certain statue. It was the Madonna of Stalingrad. In it the mother Mary wishes to protect herself against the terrors that surround her. In her bosom, encircled by her arms, sits the Child. The artist created this statue in the "hell of Stalingrad", that is, in a time of extreme danger.

At about the same time a French artist became much spoken about. He too made a statue with the motif of fear. He modelled a human forearm, the hand stretched out with palm facing upwards. In the hand was a clay ball, representing the earth, and on it two little men. He called the sculpture "La main de Dieu" — the hand of God.

These are the expressions of two Christians and

genuine artists of the feeling of fear. In the East, in Stalingrad, the utterly hopeless situation of thousands of despairing soldiers. In the West, in Paris, the falling bombs! Neither of these men was spared the experience of fear. No, their faith had to endure the test of fear. But in these troubled days and weeks, a great assurance was given them: our life is in His hands.

The follower of Jesus has this advantage over other people: he has security in the face of the threat of death, refuge with Him, permanent protection, the assurance of,

> He will bring us through!

What riches, what a treasury of faith we have in our old hymns with this glad assurance that we do not stand in a place of defeat! Amid all the confusion of our time, the Father's eye rests upon us.

> In heavenly love abiding,
> No change my heart shall fear;
> And safe is such confiding,
> For nothing changes here.
> The storm may roar without me,
> My heart may low be laid,
> But God is round about me,
> And can I be dismayed?

The way of Christ's Church will not end in darkness. With all these fears, there is another side to the coin: light and joy in fellowship with the Lord Jesus. Thus the Latin proverb holds good for us as well,

> "per angustas ad augustas"
> through narrow places into broad ones

or,

> "premor non opprimor"
> I am pressed but not to death.

Here the words of the apostle Paul are relevant (2 Cor. 6:9), "as dying, and behold we live." The world has written us off, but the Lord has written us in His book. "Even the very hairs of your head are all numbered." Therefore we do not fear.

V. THE FINAL VICTORY IS THE LORD'S

> In the Name of Jesus,
> Every knee shall bow,
> Every tongue confess Him
> King of glory now;
> 'Tis the Father's pleasure
> We should call Him Lord,
> Who from the beginning
> Was the mighty Word.

1. I have twice been to Rio de Janeiro, and each time I have marvelled at the natural beauty of this city. In stark contrast, however, to the landscape so richly endowed by its Creator, is the life and behaviour of the people who live in the place. If you have once stayed there at Carnival time, you will know that there is no possibility of comparing this with carnivals anywhere else in the world. This season of tomfoolery reaches its climax when three days and nights are given over to continuous

celebrations. The people dance with such passion and ecstasy, that one can only ask how they can physically hold out for 72 hours non-stop. It is truly a demonic secret with these Indian hybrids, how their bodies can stand being possessed with this mad spirit of dancing.

And all this is carried on under the eyes of the 100-foot statue of Christ on the Corcorado. Towering over the city stands a mountain 2,300 feet high, and its summit is crowned with this colossal statue. I was fascinated by this figure of Christ. I saw it not only when the sun was shining, but when it was raining too. The Christ was shrouded in thick clouds. I waited with my camera for a moment when the clouds would disperse a little.

This Christ standing over the metropolis has a symbolic significance. Below, the dance-mad people — above, the Christ. Below, the daily round of crimes — above, the One beneath whose eyes all these things are done. Below, chaos, turmoil, rush and hurry — above, the Silent One. Below, the situations changing from day to day — above, the One who is eternally changeless.

So Christ stands over the whole world. Below, the arena of wars and revolutions; below, love and sorrow; below, hunger and opulence — above He within whose field of vision everything happens.

He is there, even when clouds shroud Him. He is there, even though people may deny His existence. He is there, even if His presence is found uncomfortable. He has everything in His hands, even though He is silent. He Himself has borne witness to this, "All authority in heaven and on earth has been given unto me."

Christ is the plenipotentiary of God. In Him

Final Victory Is the Lord's

God's hand reaches out to us. In His hands lies the final consummation of the ways of God with mankind.

2. This victory of Jesus is already being worked out in the life of His disciples. A few years ago I held an international youth conference in France. The story of Aignes Mortes has left an unforgettable impression on my mind.

In the days of the Huguenot struggles, a 15-year-old girl was imprisoned in the tower. She would have been released at once if she had confessed allegiance to the Catholic Church. But she remained faithful to her Lord Jesus, and would not be moved. For 38 years she wasted away in the dungeon. At the age of 53 she was released. What victorious power there is in the name of Jesus, that a tender girl could allow herself to be imprisoned 38 years for His sake!

The same victory is evident today in Red China and in other parts of the world. Mao Tse-tung commands a huge empire. Millions are under his control. There is however one limit to his power — the Christian faith of the disciples of Jesus. There are some gaining the victory in Red China whose motto might be summed up in the verse from Luther's hymn:

> Let goods and kindred go,
> This mortal life also;
> The body they may kill —
> God's truth abideth still,
> His kingdom is for ever.

Ever since the cross of Calvary was set up on this earth as a sign of victory, there have been those who were ready to pay every price to remain loyal to it.

The example which has both shocked and encouraged me more than any other in the last few years has been that of Jim Roger. He was working in the Congo at a time when rebels were killing off the Belgian and American missionaries. As a Scot, Jim was not included on the black list. His sick friend and brother Bill, on the other hand, was an American, and was to be killed as a hostage. Jim remained loyal to his sick brother and accompanied him to his death.

Here the victory of Jesus shines through. And if we mortals were able to hear the fanfares of victory in the heavenly realm, the sound would fill the whole world. He whose ears the Holy Spirit has opened hears the shouts of jubilation from those who love the cross of Jesus and await the Lord's coming.

3. This victory will one day be made manifest for all to see. At present His power and authority are hidden from the view of the world. The time of concealment will come to an end, when the concentration of power in the hands of the Antichrist has reached its climax here on earth.

One event in history seems to me a symbol of the final victory of the Lord Jesus. When Ferdinand Cortez, the Spanish conqueror, was fighting with the Aztecs, his troops were almost exterminated. The Aztecs fought with true Indian valour. In the end Cortez was left with a handful of his most loyal men, while on the other side there was a vastly superior force, of 22,000 Aztec warriors. The Spaniards' cause seemed lost and hopeless. Then Cortez staked everything on one last bid. Near the

Final Fictory Is the Lord's

enemy's standards he caught sight of the Aztec leader. Cortez chose out his most valiant men. They galloped straight for the Aztec chief. They killed him, took the standards and flourished them before the startled Aztecs. That was the turning-point which led to victory.

Every illustration fails, in that it cannot bring out the full meaning of Scripture. This historical incident should certainly not be pressed as an analogy. The *tertium comparationis*, that is, the point of comparison, is in the fact that those who thought they had the victory in their pocket were rudely awakened. Those whose cause seemed lost, on the other hand, fought and won a total victory in the enemy's camp.

In the world, the cause of Jesus also seems to be lost. There is, in all the chaos which surrounds us, scarcely anything to be seen of His supreme power. The powers opposing Christ are continually on the advance. It is becoming dark on the earth, darker and darker. The coming Antichrist seems to have all the odds in his favour. And into the midst of this vastly superior force the returning Lord will come, to snatch the victory from those who are so confident of it.

> Look, ye saints, the sight is glorious,
> See the "Man of Sorrows" now
> From the fight return victorious:
> Every knee to Him shall bow!

4. The Church of Christ has no reason to be afraid. The future does not lie in Russia's or Red China's hands. It does not lie in the hands of the Pope or the Antichrist, nor of the devil and the demons.

The future belongs to the crucified, descended, risen, ascended and returning Lord.

Isaiah rejoices in prophetic vision, "The government is on his shoulder." Paul triumphs in the words, "God has bestowed on him the name which is above every name."

"All his enemies to be a footstool for his feet!"

That is the last, great victory of the Coming One. When the earth is writhing under a thousand pains, and humanity bleeding from a million wounds, authority will be handed over to the One who was rejected by mankind at Calvary.

Meanwhile we look for the promised Day X. This day will not be produced by the natural rush of uncontrollable events here on earth. Nor will it be brought on by the hopes and longings of believers. Day X is a predetermined day, an act of God. He will decide when it is to come.

Day X is the day of salvation for the Church.

Day X is the day of judgment for the world. This is no gloating on the part of the followers of Jesus, but the order of events decided by the Creator and Ruler of this world. This Day X will not fail to come. It is approaching. Anyone of spiritual discernment is aware that the heavenly hosts are already getting ready for the great day. How blessed we are to have such a mighty Lord, who will come and put an end to all sorrow!

VI. WHO WILL TAKE PART?

On a missionary journey in Africa, I was once involved in a little incident which makes a good

Who Will Take Part?

parable. Travelling from Johannesburg, I had to change planes in Nairobi, and as the next flight to Aden was not until the next day, I had to put up for the night in a hotel there. I did not take all my luggage with me for the one night, but left it at the airport. It was quite bad enough to have to drag myself along with my suitcase in the African heat. At the hotel I was the guest of the airline with which I had made my booking. I had, however, an unpleasant surprise when the gong for dinner was sounded in the evening: I was not allowed into the dining room in my travelling clothes. I was told I must wear a dark suit. I explained that I had left my dark suit with my luggage at the airport. It was all to no avail: they would not let me in. I demanded to be allowed to see the hotel proprietor. He was not available. Then I asked, "Then serve me my dinner in another room, if the etiquette here is so strict." That too was refused. It was an annoying experience which I took a long time to get over.

Yet today I am glad that it happened to me. I had received a splendid object-lesson about a certain piece of teaching in the New Testament. In Matthew 22 we are told the story of the royal marriage. In verses 11 and 12 it says,

"But when the king came in to look at the guests, he saw there a man who had no wedding-garment; and he said to him, 'Friend, how did you get in here without a wedding-garment?' And he was speechless."

Here we have an answer to the question at the head of this chapter, "Who will be in on the victory of Jesus?" Only he who comes with a "wedding-garment" will partake of the glory of the Kingdom of God. This term requires some explanation.

The story of the Prodigal Son in Luke 15 tells us what we are to understand by this "wedding-garment". When the son had returned, dirty and in rags, the father said to his servants (15:22), "Bring quickly the best robe, and put it on him!" This did not happen until the son had confessed, "Father, I have sinned against heaven and before you; I am no longer worthy to be called your son." After the recognition and confession of his guilt, the returning prodigal was dressed in the festal robe.

This parable teaches us that unforgiven sin bars the way into the glory of God. Forgiven sin, however, opens the gate to the Father's house.

The New Testament emphasizes this truth in many ways. In Revelation 7:14 the exalted Lord says, "These are they who have come out of the great tribulation; they have washed their robes and made them white in the blood of the Lamb."

The blood of Jesus allows us to enter glory.

The blood of Jesus is the sign that on Calvary God has judged the sin of the world and our sin. The blood of Jesus is the sign that on Calvary God has forgiven our sin. The blood is the sign that God has sanctified us through the sacrifice of Jesus (Heb. 10:14). The blood of Jesus is the password, by which we find entrance into the Father's Kingdom.

Only those who are cleansed through the blood of Jesus will experience fellowship with the exalted and returning Lord. The Lord says this in Rev. 3:4, "They have not soiled their garments; and they shall walk with me in white, for they are worthy." "White garments", the "wedding garment", the "festal robe", are found only at the foot of the cross. Since a different doctrine of the cross is being disseminated by false teachers, we must repeat what

Who Will Take Part?

we mean by the cross. The cross is for us the reality of Jesus' death, where He died as the Son of God for our sins and through it purged them.

Who will take part? we ask again. Once again we will take up the historical illustration from the last chapter. When Cortez had killed the Aztec chieftain by a bold venture, the few loyal ones who had dared to go with him were the ones who shared the fruits of his victory.

When Jesus comes again and sets up His Kingdom, only those few will be "in on it" who have dared to go with Him. It is only a small company, but theirs is the inheritance. "Fear not, little flock, for it is your Father's good pleasure to give you the kingdom." This promise is firmer than heaven and earth. And we share its permanence.

Only the blood-bought Church of the Lord will inherit the kingdom.

We will close this chapter and the book by relating a little incident. It was a great privilege for me to be invited some years ago by Wilhelm Busch to conduct a campaign in Essen. This master among evangelists was an example to me in many things. I gained much from the eight days of working together with him. Being together with him each day, I learned several things from his life and work. Among other things he recounted to me a dream, which I shall never forget. I am not a great lover of dreams: I prefer the word of God. But there is such a thing as a God-given dream. In his dream, Wilhelm Busch saw himself in a great hall in heaven. An angel said to him, "Here is a file with the names of all who are saved." Wilhelm Busch was given permission to look through it. Naturally he looked under B. In his search he discovered three things. Busch related,

"Firstly I was surprised to find the names of some people there, of whom I would never have thought that they were saved. Then, to my dismay, I could not see some of the names I should have expected to find. And thirdly I was most amazed of all to find my own name among the saved."

Is our name among the saved? Are we in God's file? If so, can we know that we are? Yes! John writes (1 John 5:12, 13), "He who has the Son has life . . . I write this to you who believe in the name of the Son of God, that you may know that you have eternal life."

You may know that you have eternal life! Something we can know and have, not by our own worthiness or deserving, but by His grace alone. It is not our work, but His, His alone! To Him be the glory for ever and ever!